beyond graffiti ?

"Graffiti" is a term generally used to denote 'street art', albeit a very particular type of street art called "tags", names, mostly, of a street gang, or the artist, spray painted on walls in bright colors and dynamic letters, like used for action comic books. This book includes interesting examples of these "tags", plus shows examples of a great many other types of street art, some of the most interesting and unusual art produced on building walls, in America, during the past ten years of this twentieth century.

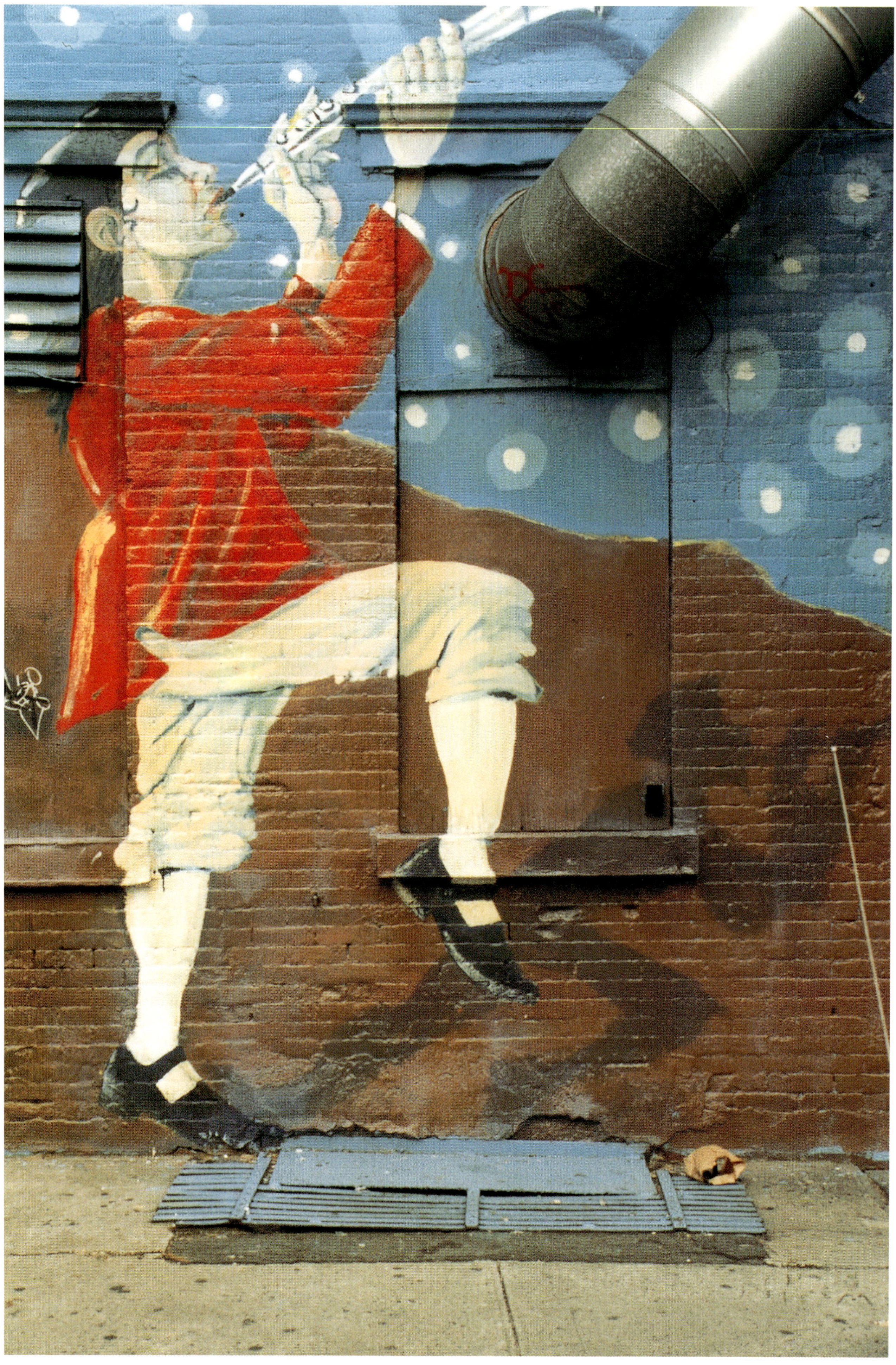

new AMERICAN STREET ART

Photography by Bob Edelson

A SOHO BOOK PROJECT

*This book is dedicated
to the many excellent artists
who have difficulty reaching an audience,
or obtaining sufficient remuneration for their art to go on,
yet, who do go on, contributing, in some way, great or small,
to making our lives worth living.*

INTRODUCTION

Street art, to my way of thinking, is the most exciting of all graphic art. Of course, I'm speaking of 'good' street art. There's all kinds of street art just as there's all kinds of any other art, as you'll see in this book (though we've only included the really good stuff). What we have included represents the most interesting and diverse examples I've been fortunate to discover and photograph in various urban communities around the U.S. the past 10 years. Most come from New York City and Miami, not because street art is better or more abundant in these cities, but because I spend most of my time in them. I find street art in just about every city I visit, and have included some wonderful examples from Los Angeles, Key West, New Orleans, and Montreal, Canada, just not as much, because my time in these cities was limited.

It takes a lot of time wandering city streets to discover good street art. It isn't exactly everywhere, and, wherever it's been, it's likely gone by now. Almost all street art is short-lived, gone within days or certainly weeks after it is completed, either because it will be washed or painted over, or the wall it's on could be torn down. (I doubt there's more than a handful of the works in this book that still exists other than as a photograph). A street art work might appear on a street one day, disappear the next, and if you weren't there at the right time, you missed it, and there is no telling when another will appear on that street, again. So, it takes wandering a city's streets, many in not so pretty neighborhoods, many times, for a long time, to generate even a modest size collection; it'd pretty much have to come from a city you live in. And I think you'd have to, like me, enjoy wandering city streets.

When you make a discovery of street art, especially if it is both 'good' and unique, it can be an overwhelming experience. Since you're never really sure when or where you'll make such a discovery, it almost always comes unexpected, so it hits you as a visual surprise, a dazzling visual surprise; dazzling, because of the combination of dynamic, well-executed graphic, the wall it is painted on, the texture of the wall, and the entire, usually seedy, street setting, all of it, coming at you, all at once.

The artists who produce street art are, indeed, 'artists', though of a certain ilk. They learn their craft like other graphic artists, somewhere, somehow, and when they think they're ready, they want the world to see what they can do, but now. They have no patience for gallery games, or commercial constraints, so they take their quite individual passions directly to the public, right out on the street, certain their labors of love will not survive, sometimes even risking the law. And like great jazz artists, these yardbirds of color and form must improvise to fit their art to the beat of whatever wall and street they find to play.

' talkin' 'bout angel head hipsters paintin' beauty on bleak urban streets, invited or not, sometimes blowin' cool, sometimes red hot, and when it's good, there's nothing else like it, cause they give it all they got.'

I hope, as you turn each of the following pages of this book, you can imagine how each street art gem shown first appeared to me, in it's environment (street settings are often included), as big as life, so you sense the same excitement that I did.

Bob Edelson

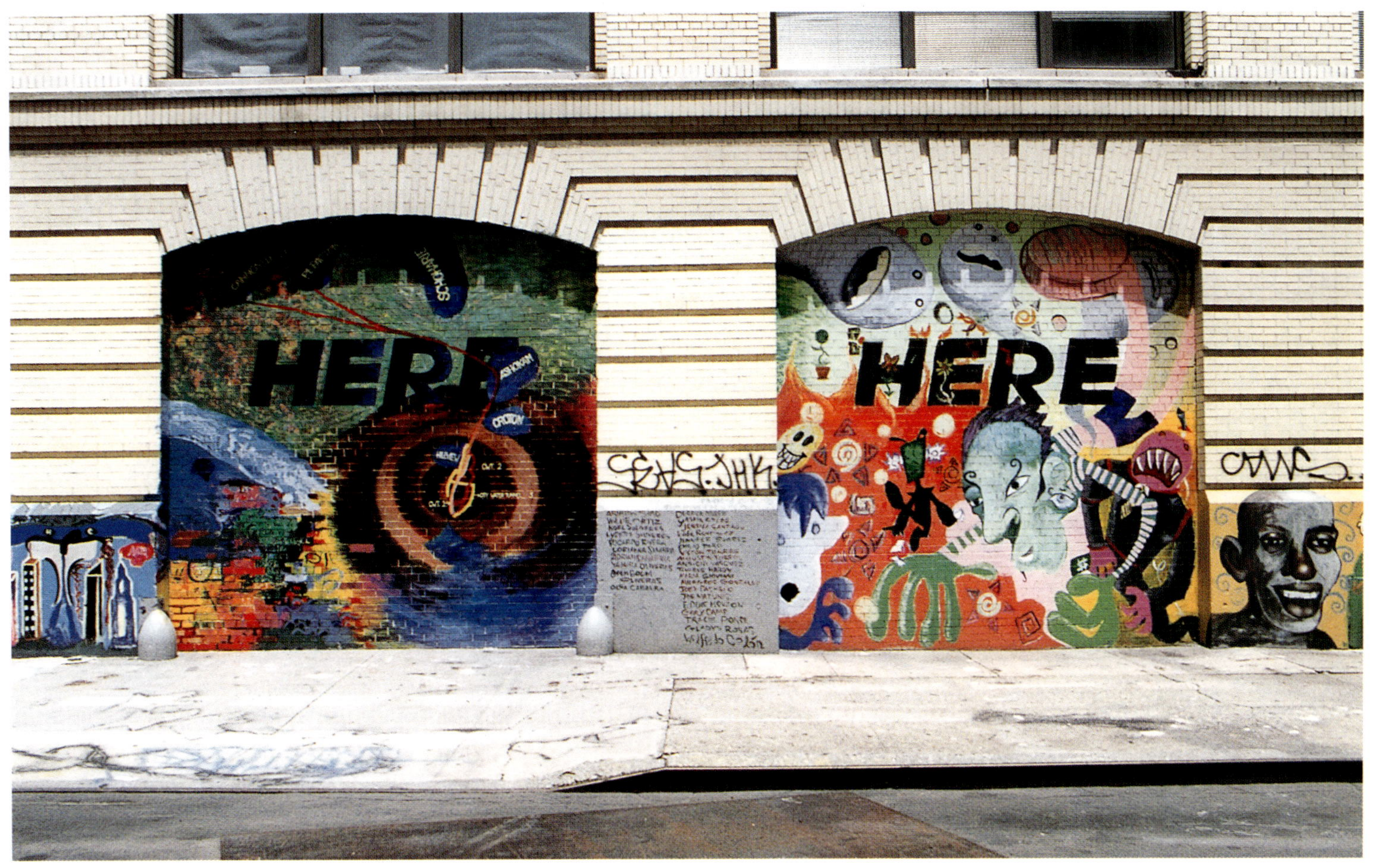

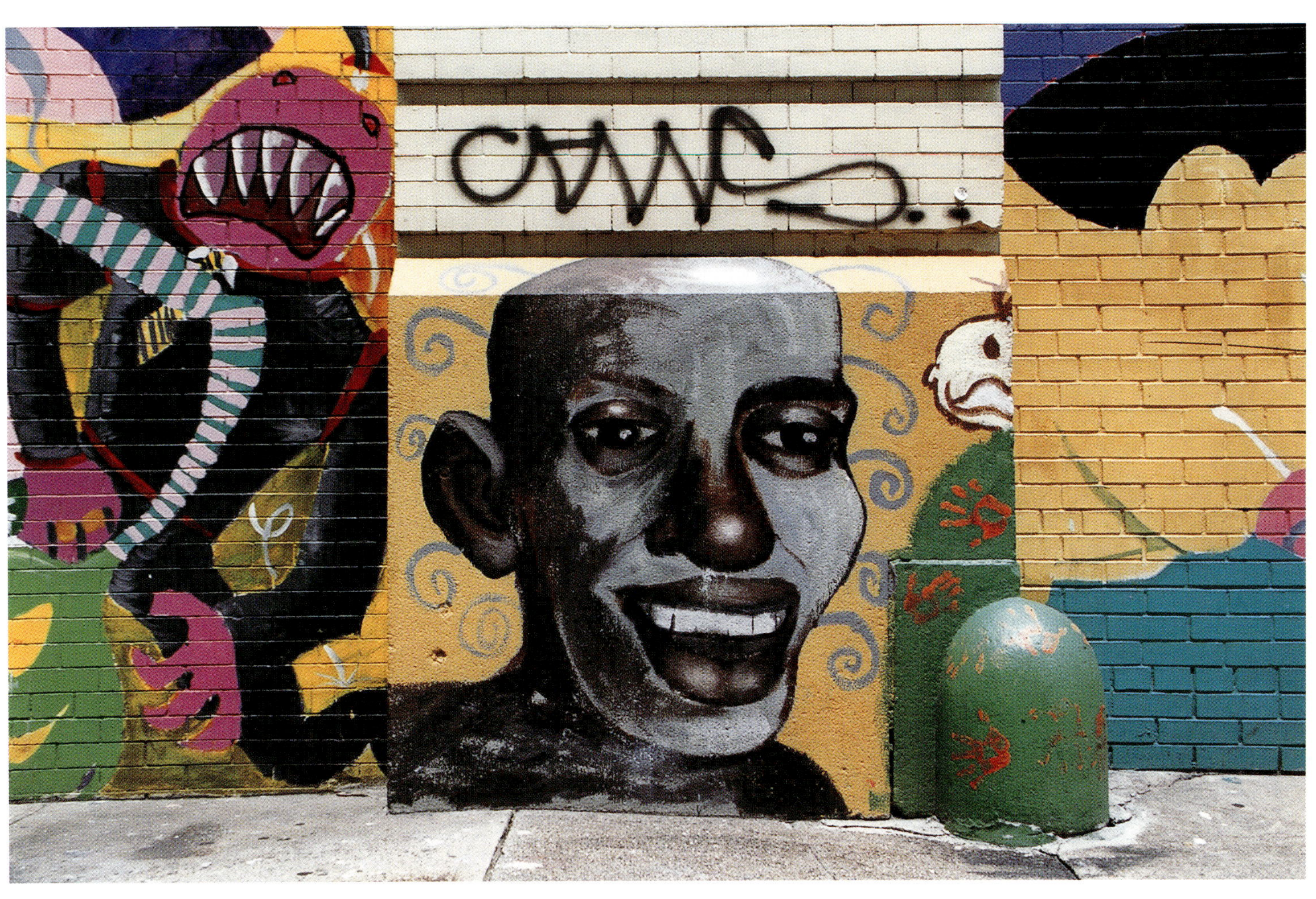

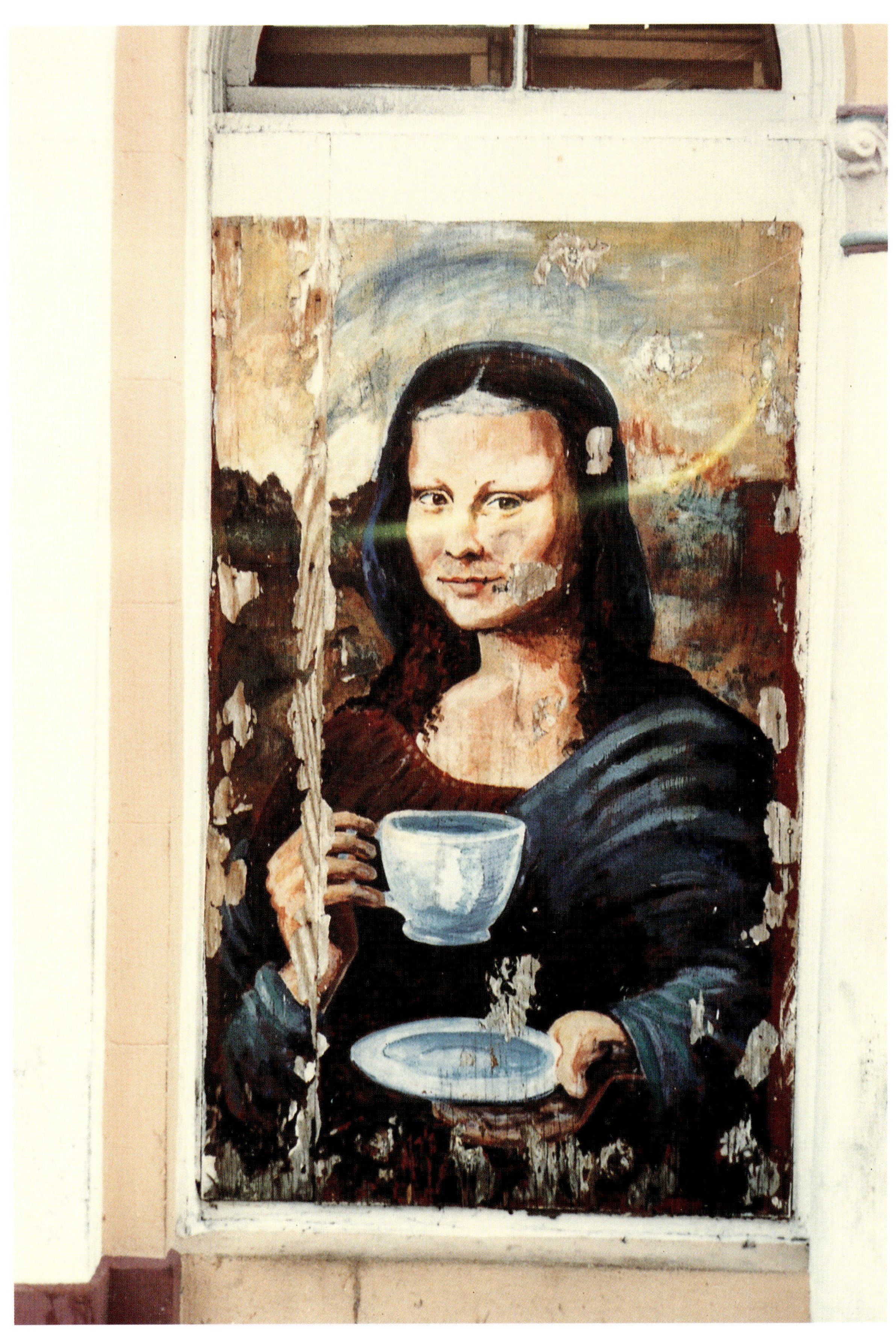

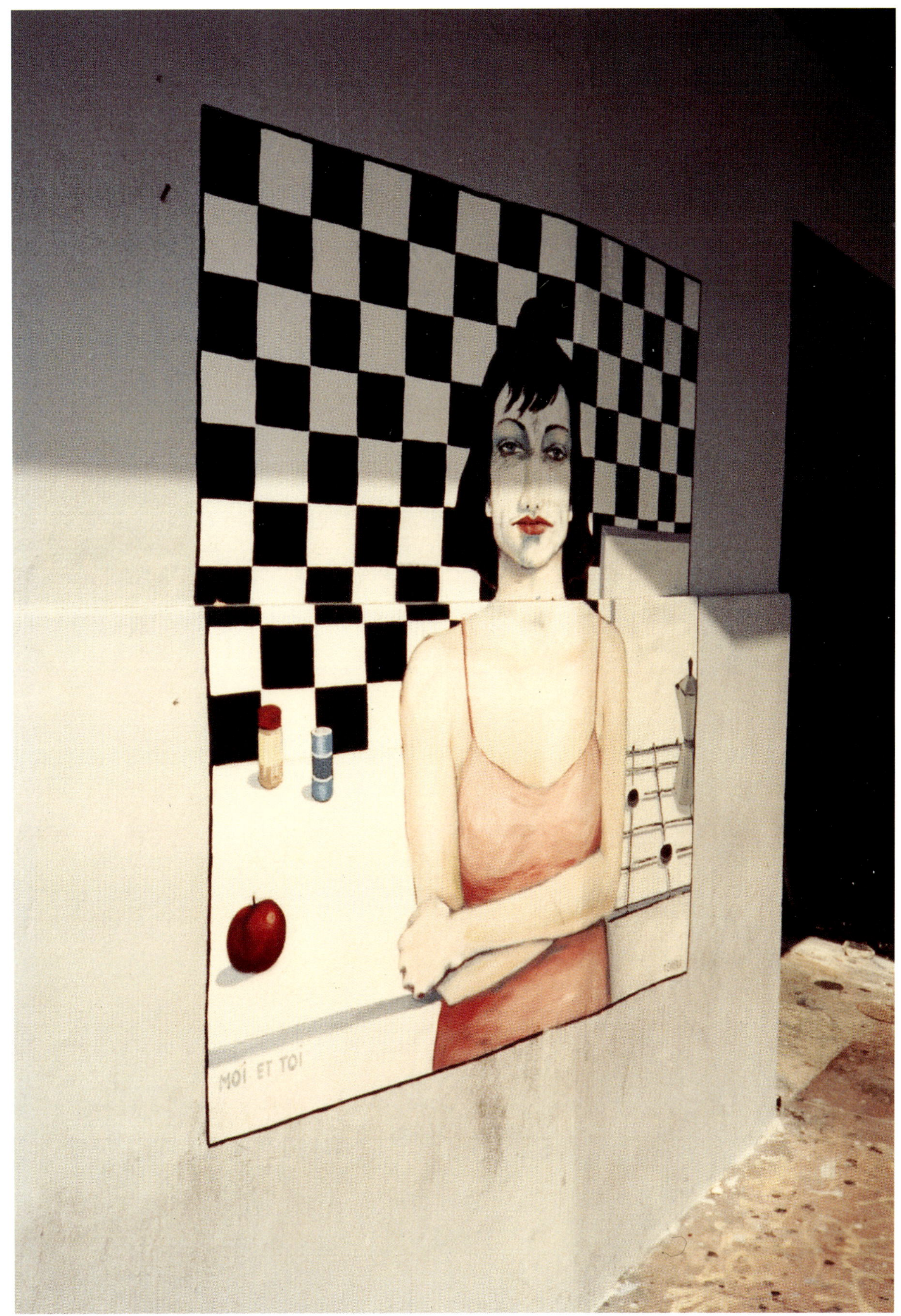

MOI ET TOI

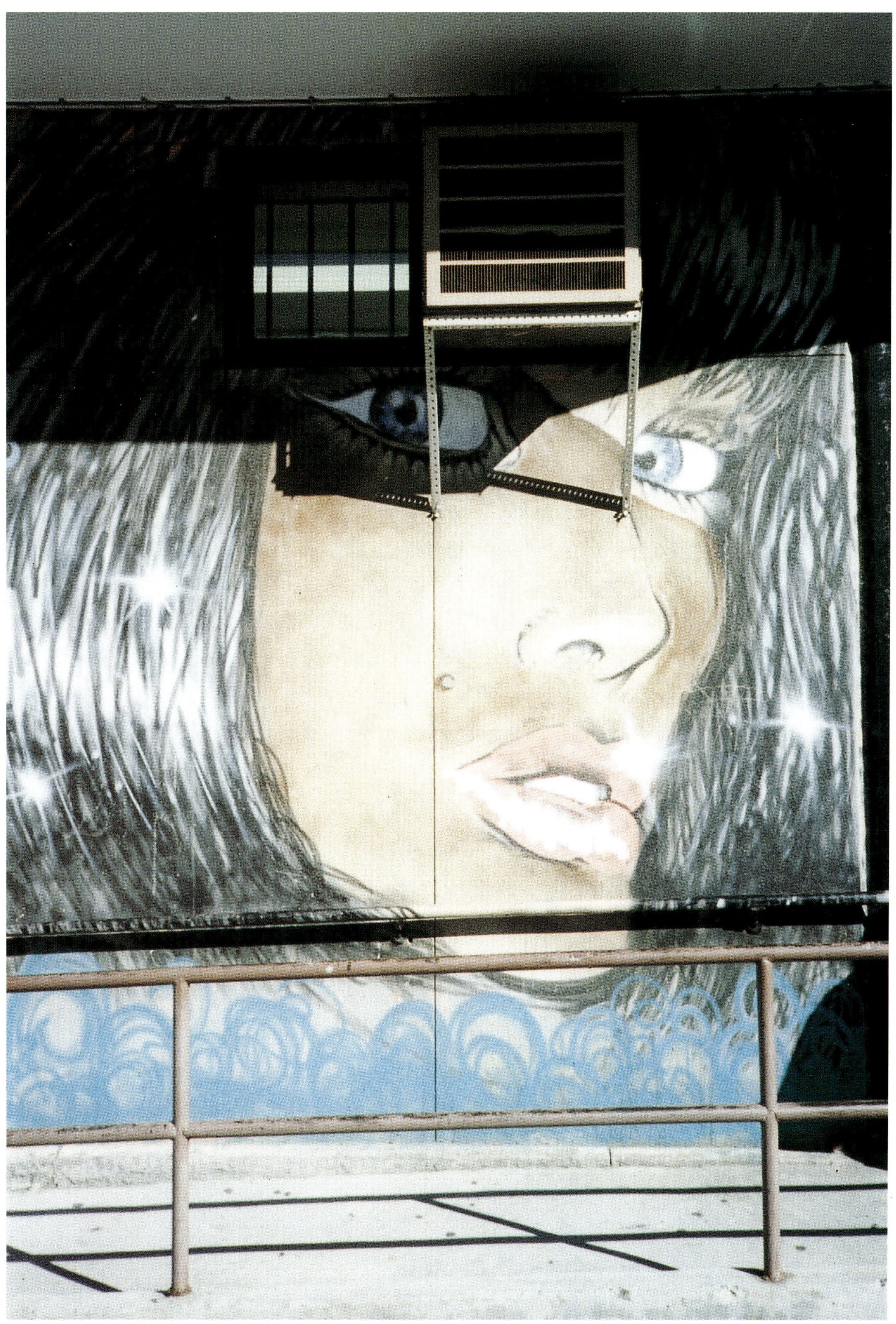

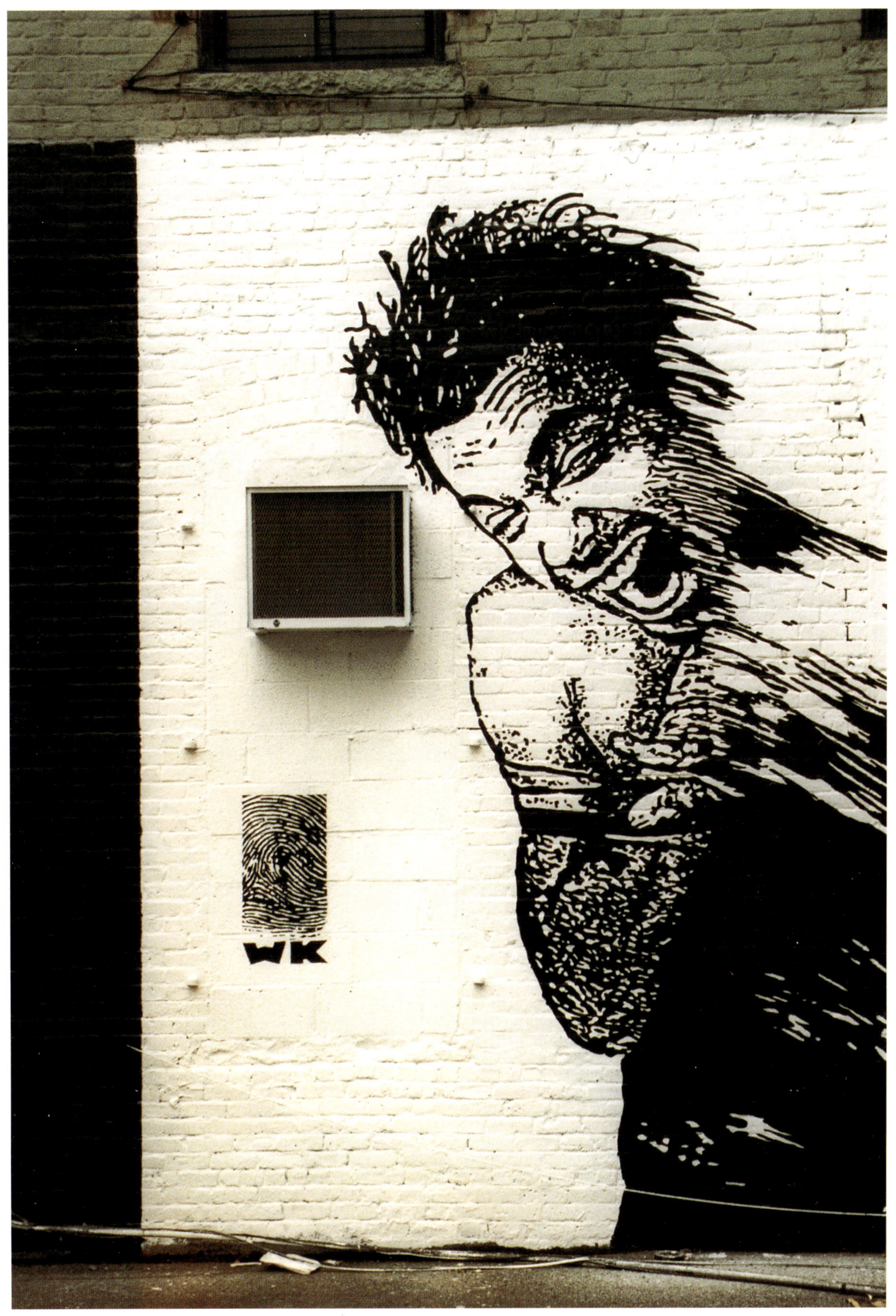

WK

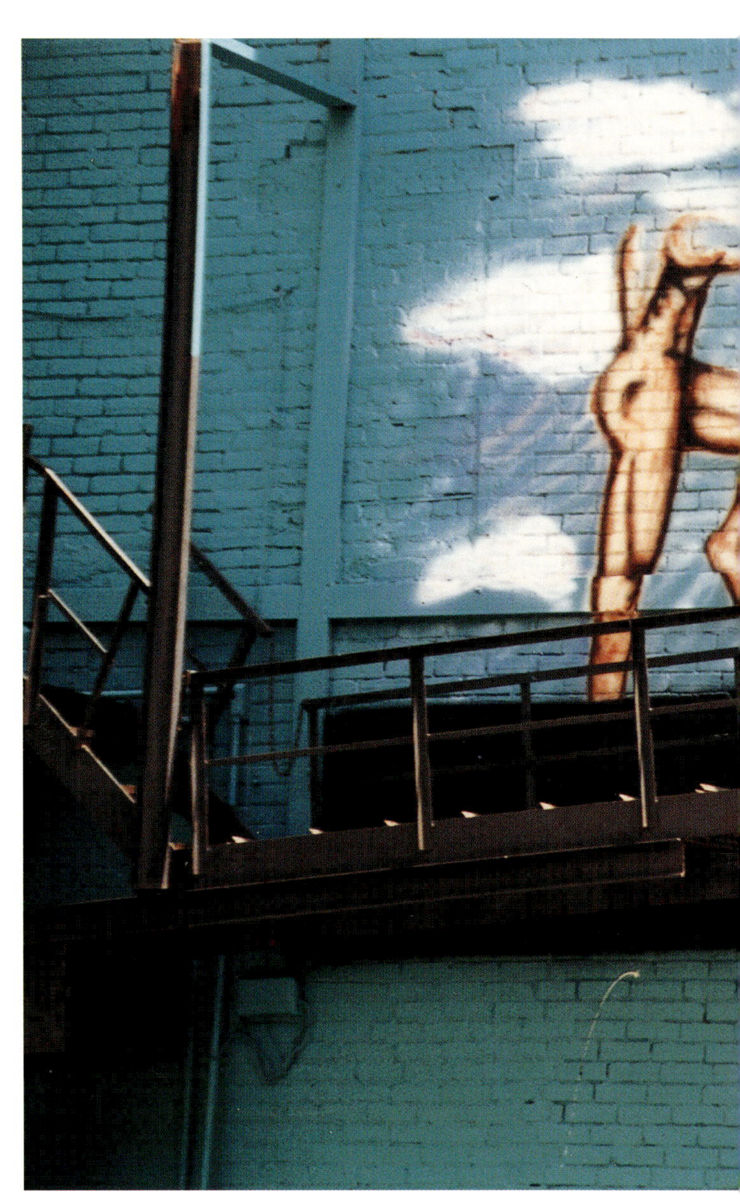

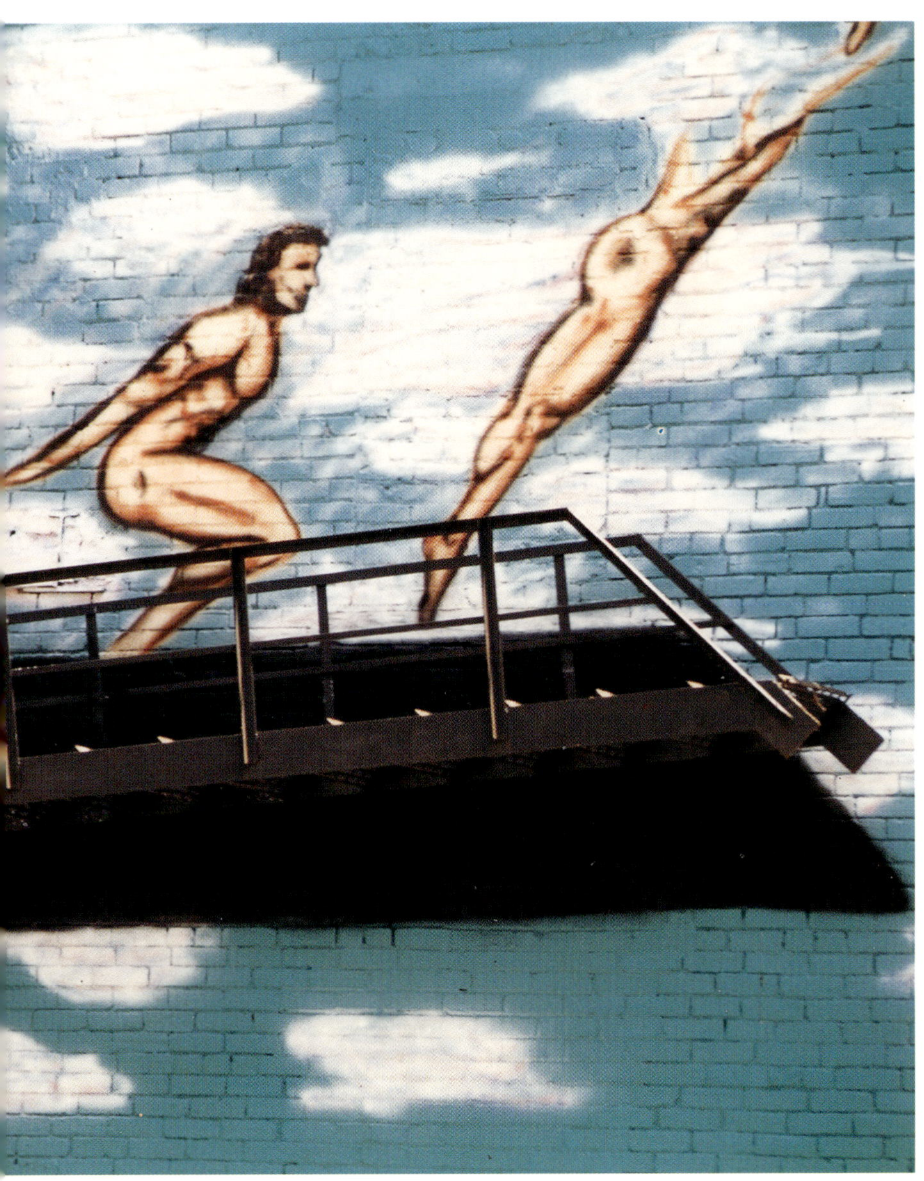

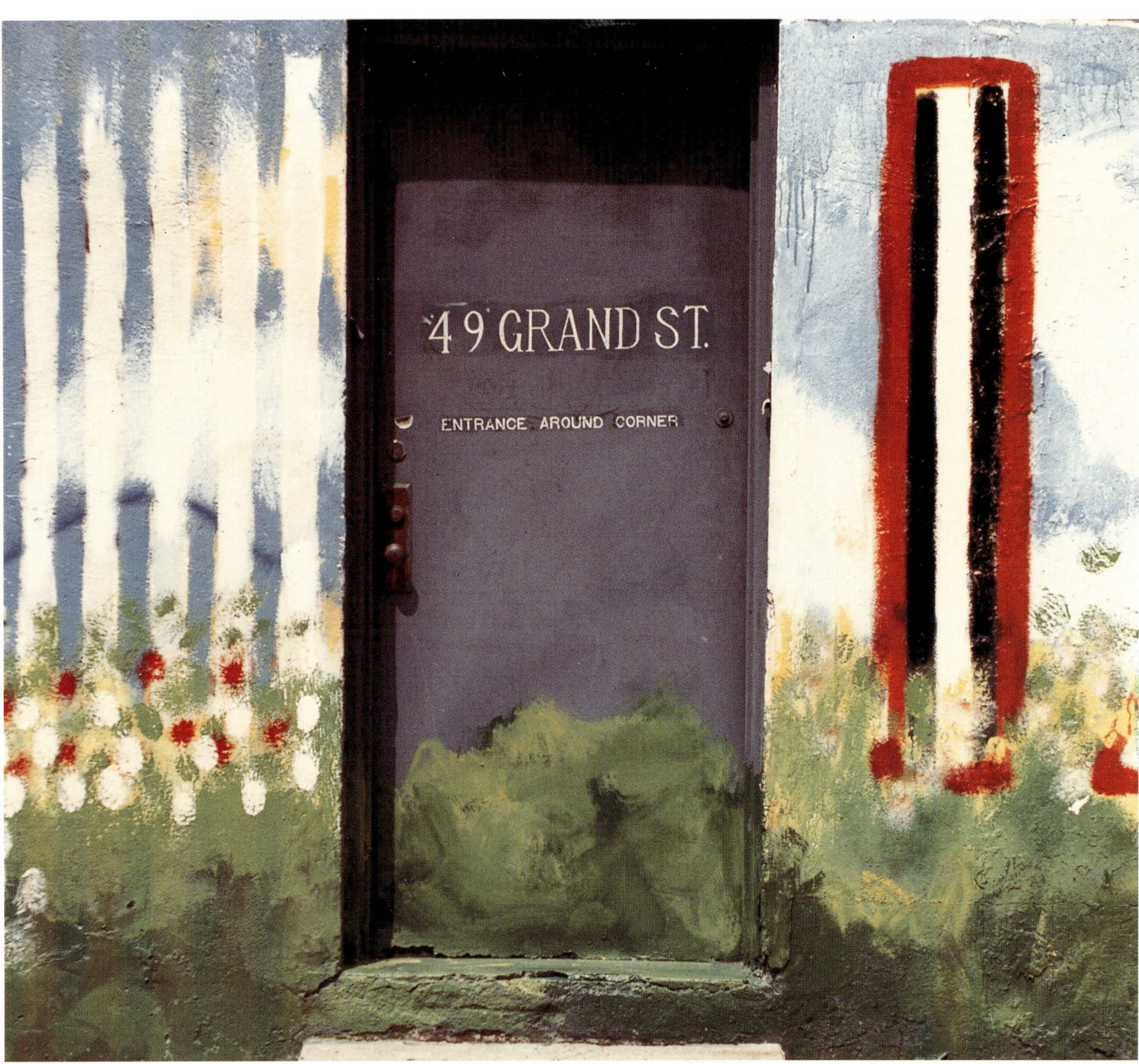
49 GRAND ST.
ENTRANCE AROUND CORNER

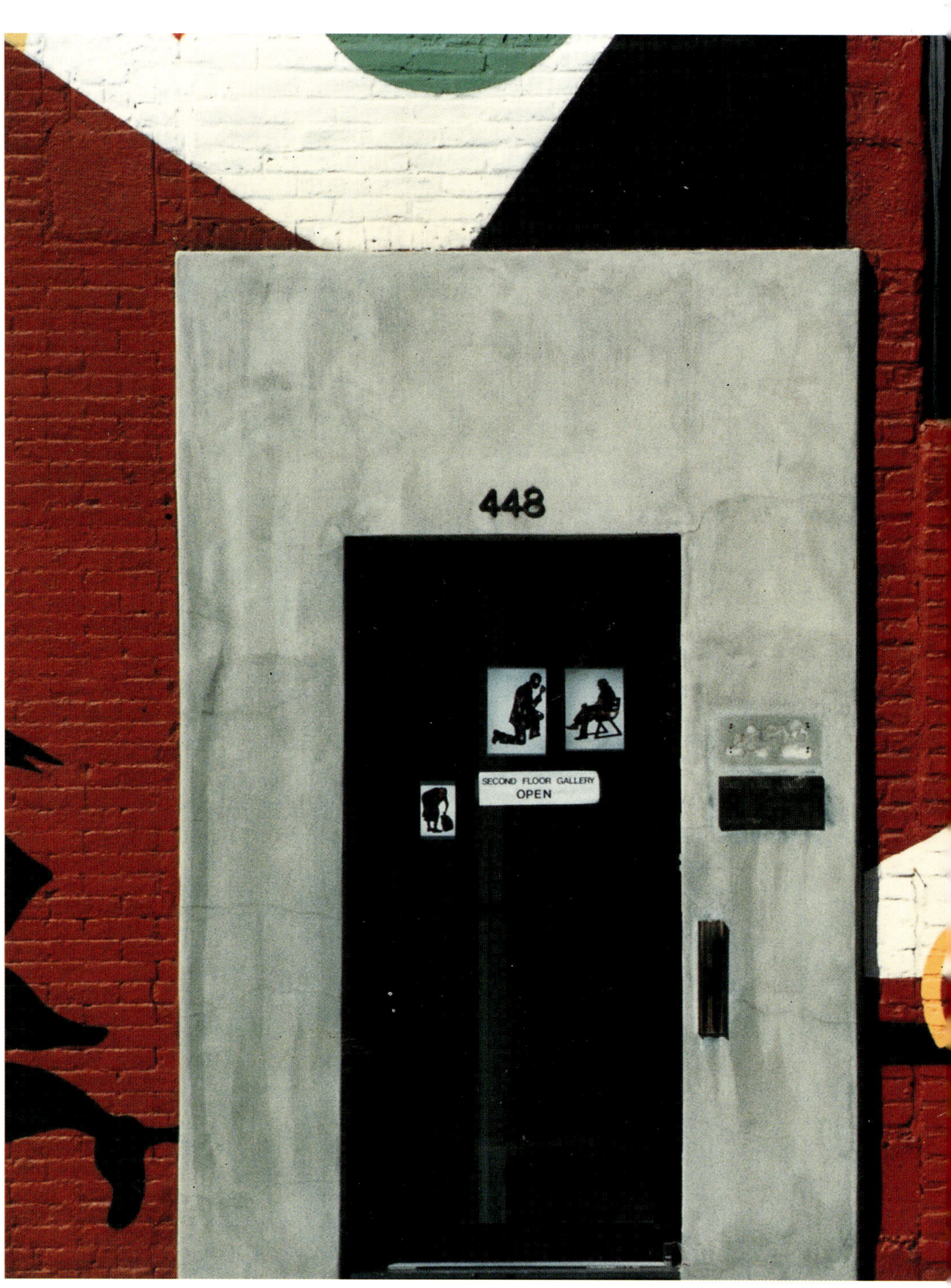

448
SECOND FLOOR GALLERY
OPEN

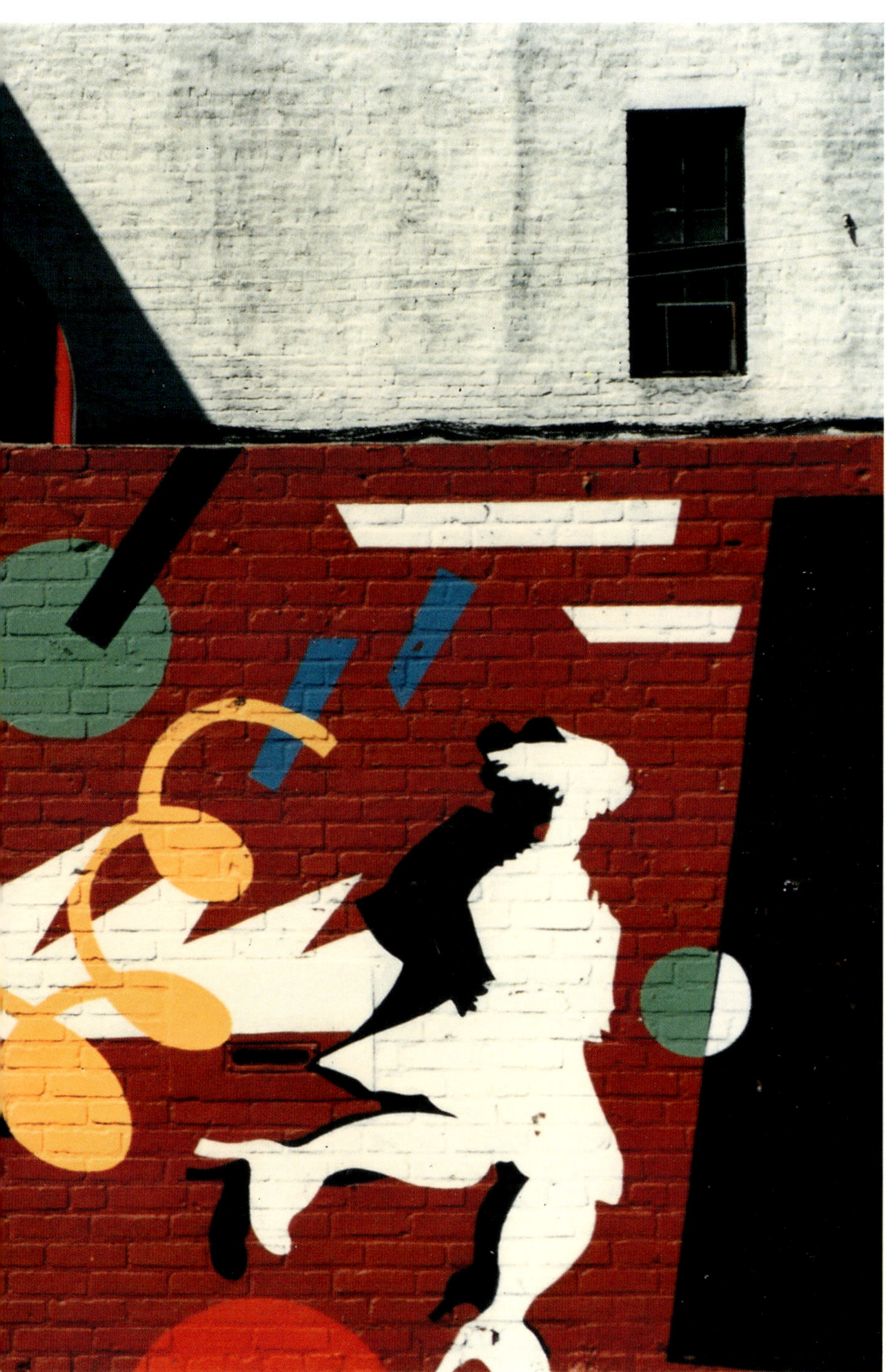

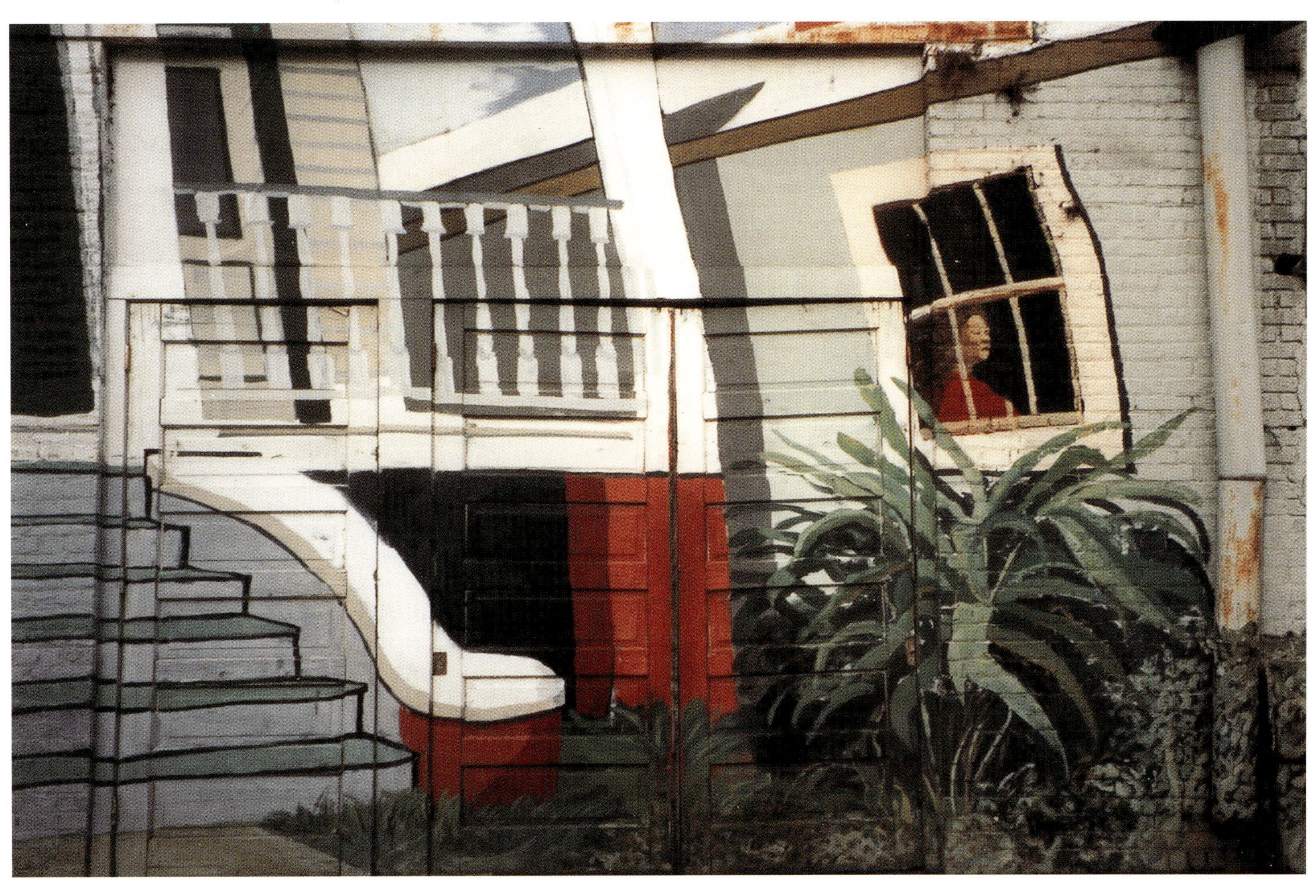

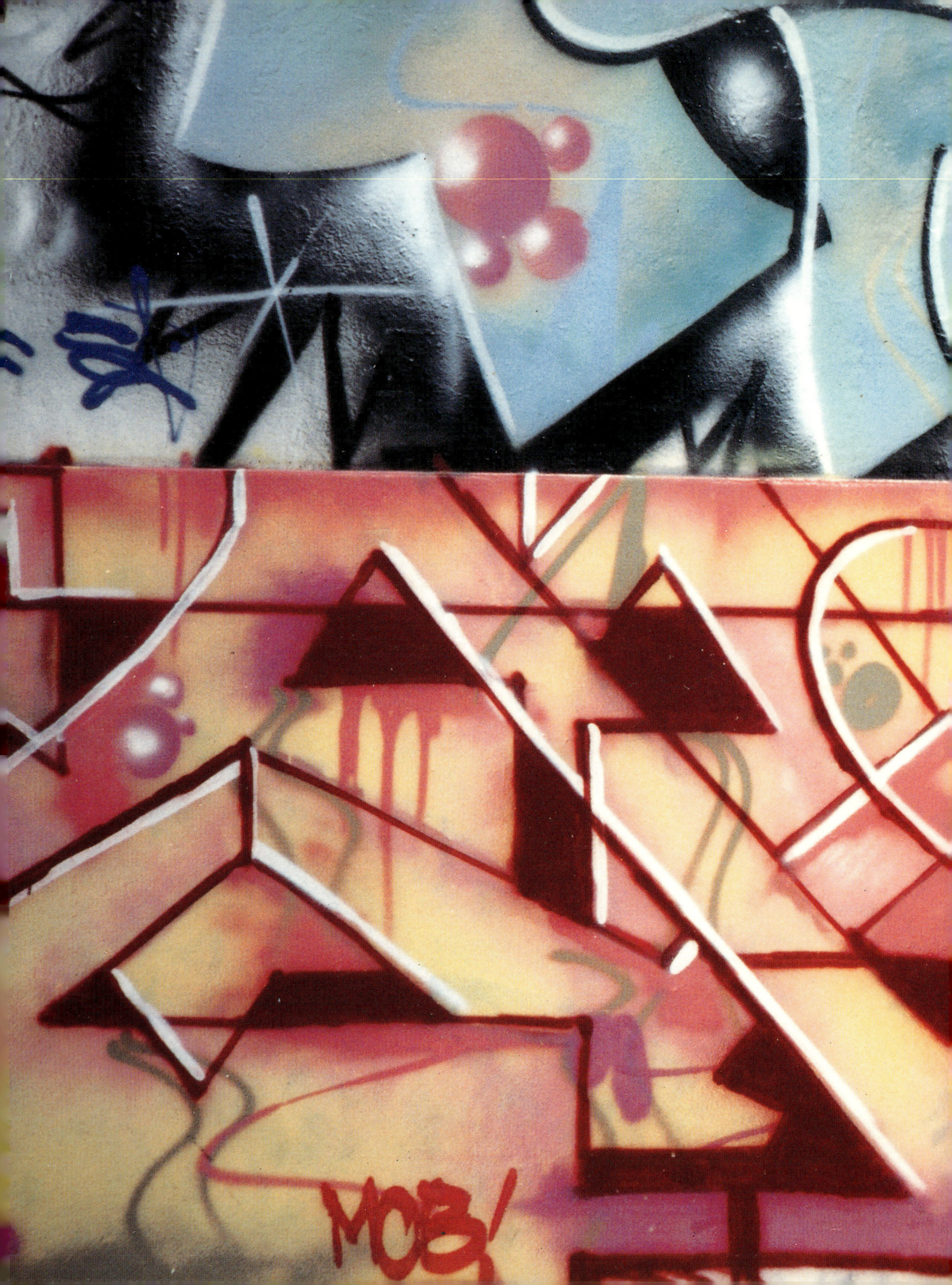
MOB!

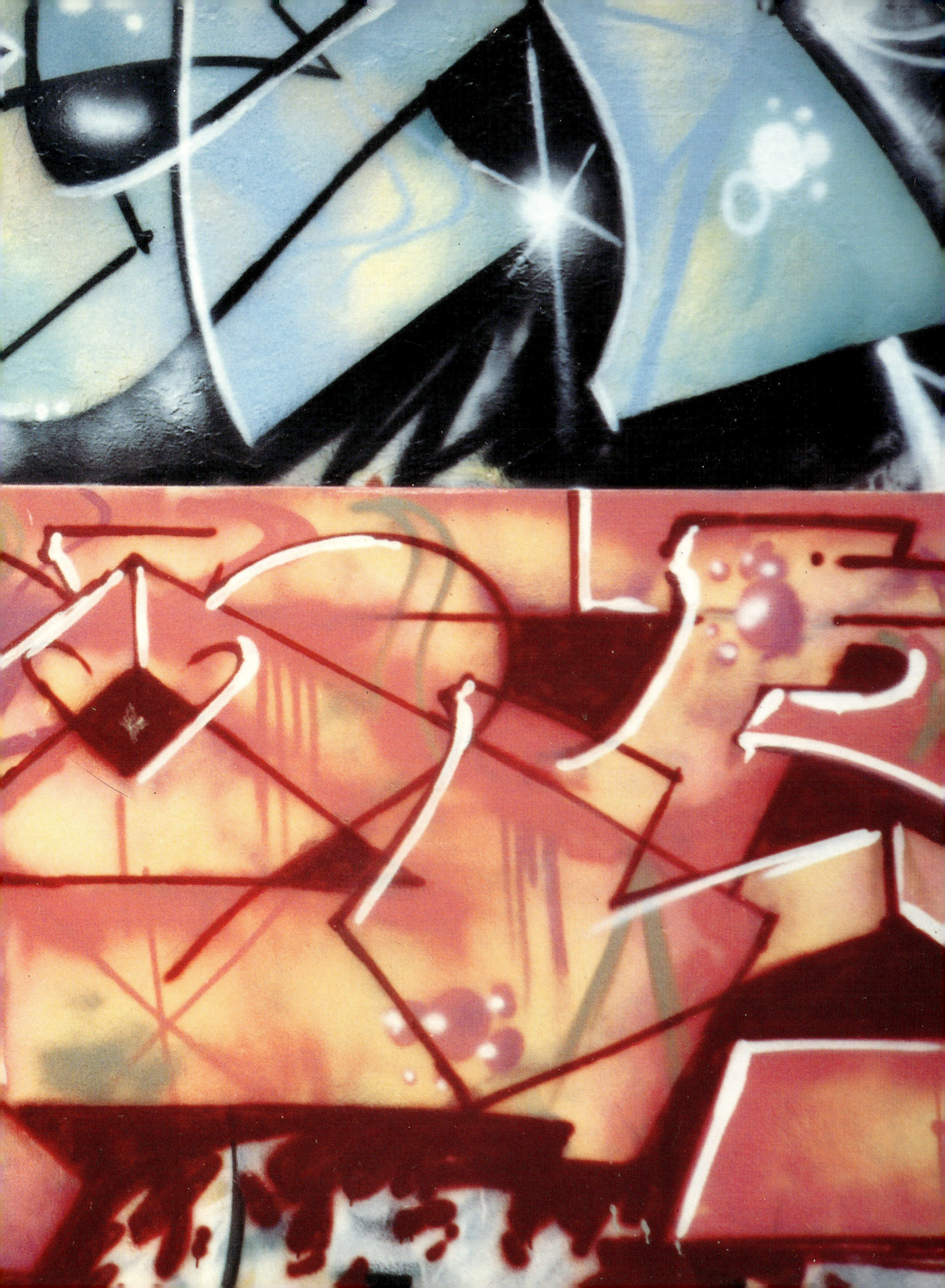

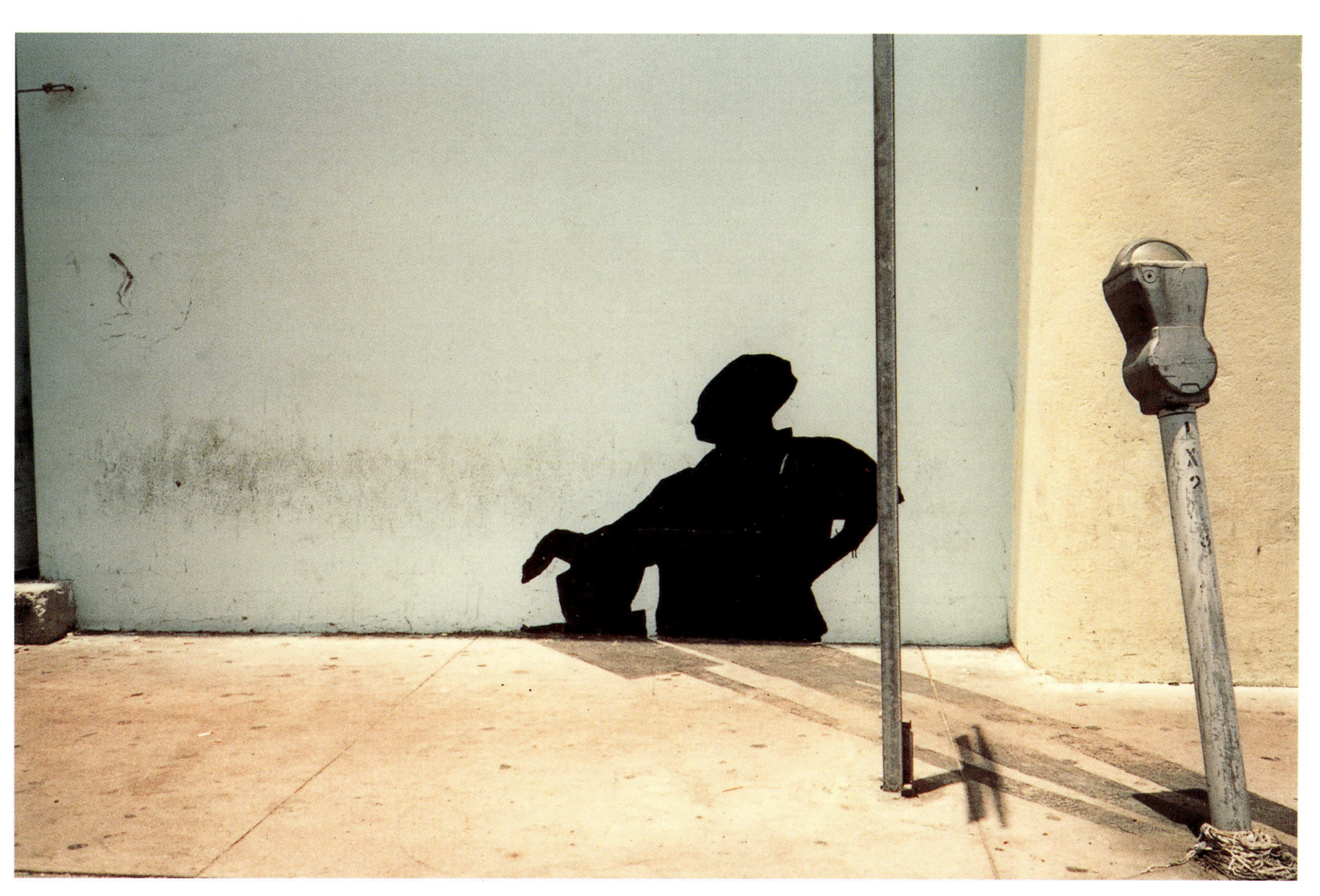

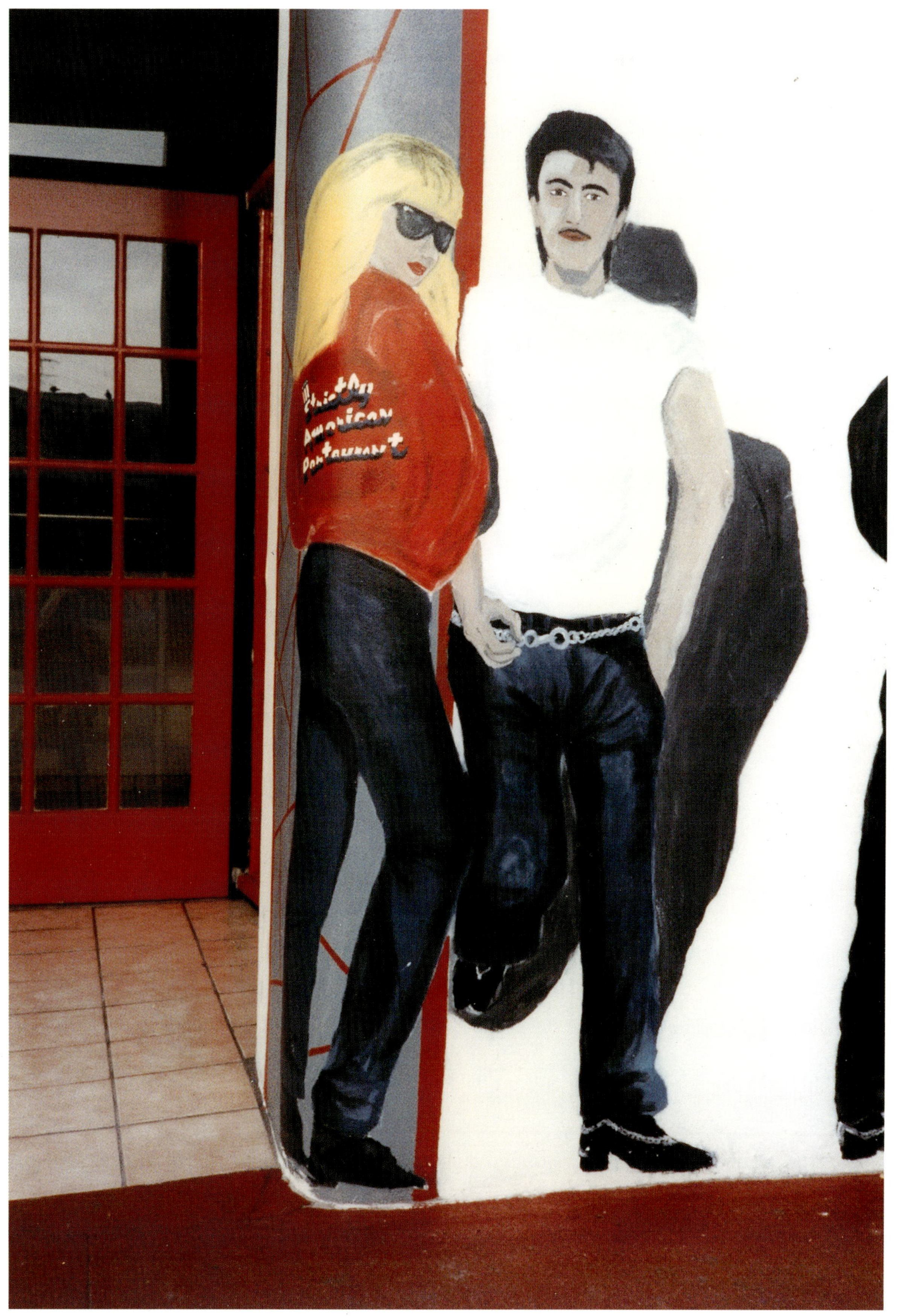

Strictly
American
Restaurant

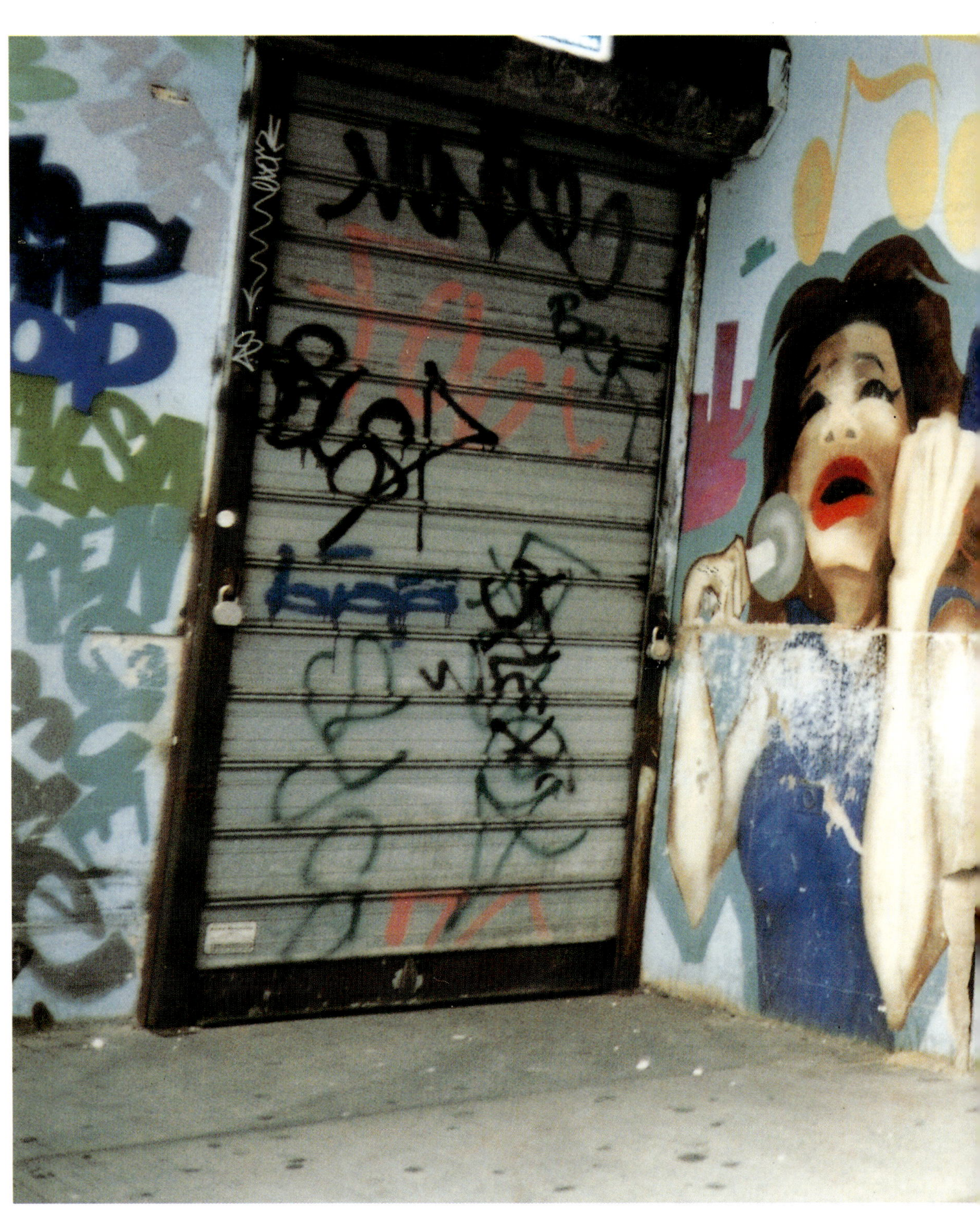

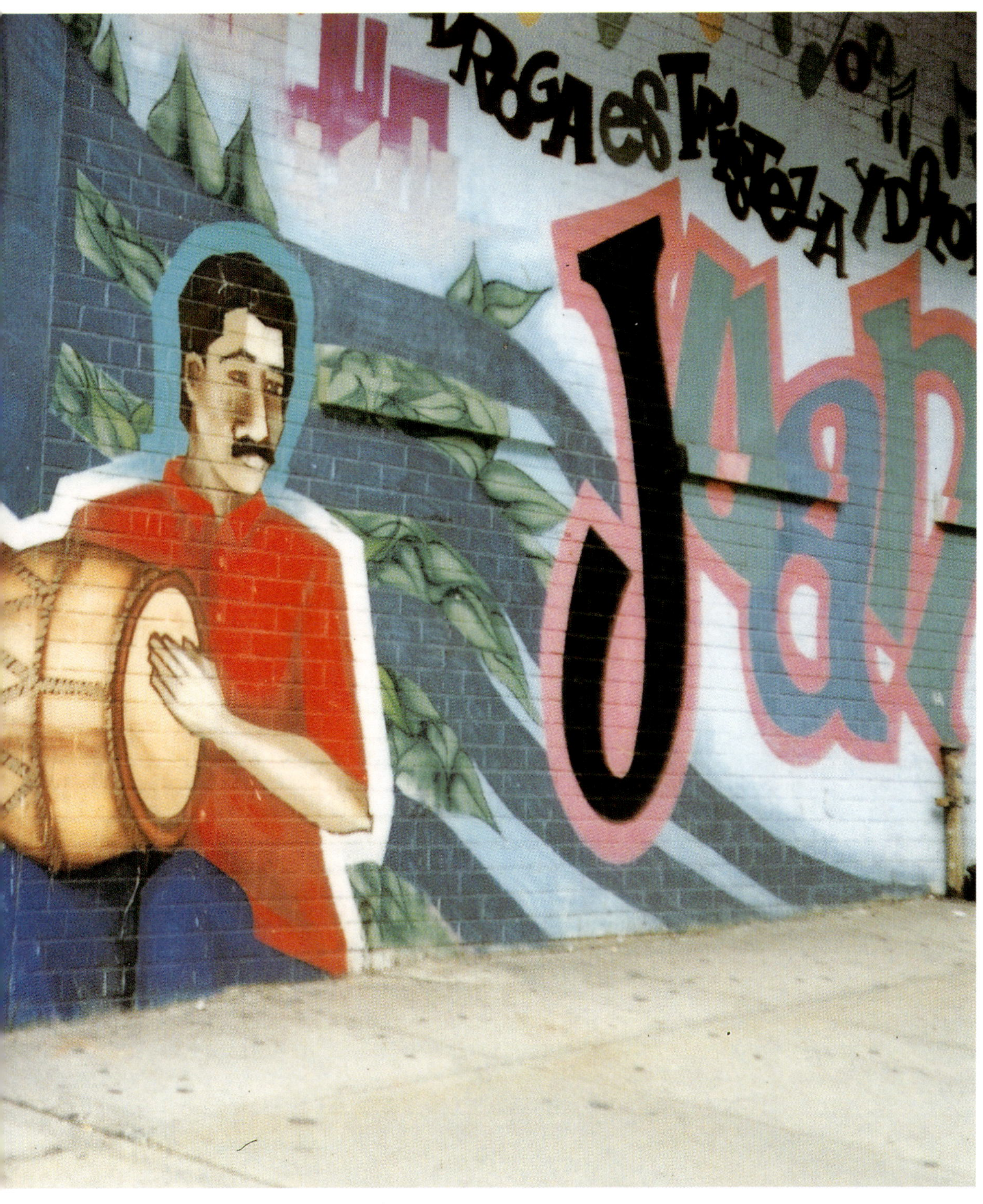
DROGA ES TRISTEZA Y DOLOR
Jaz

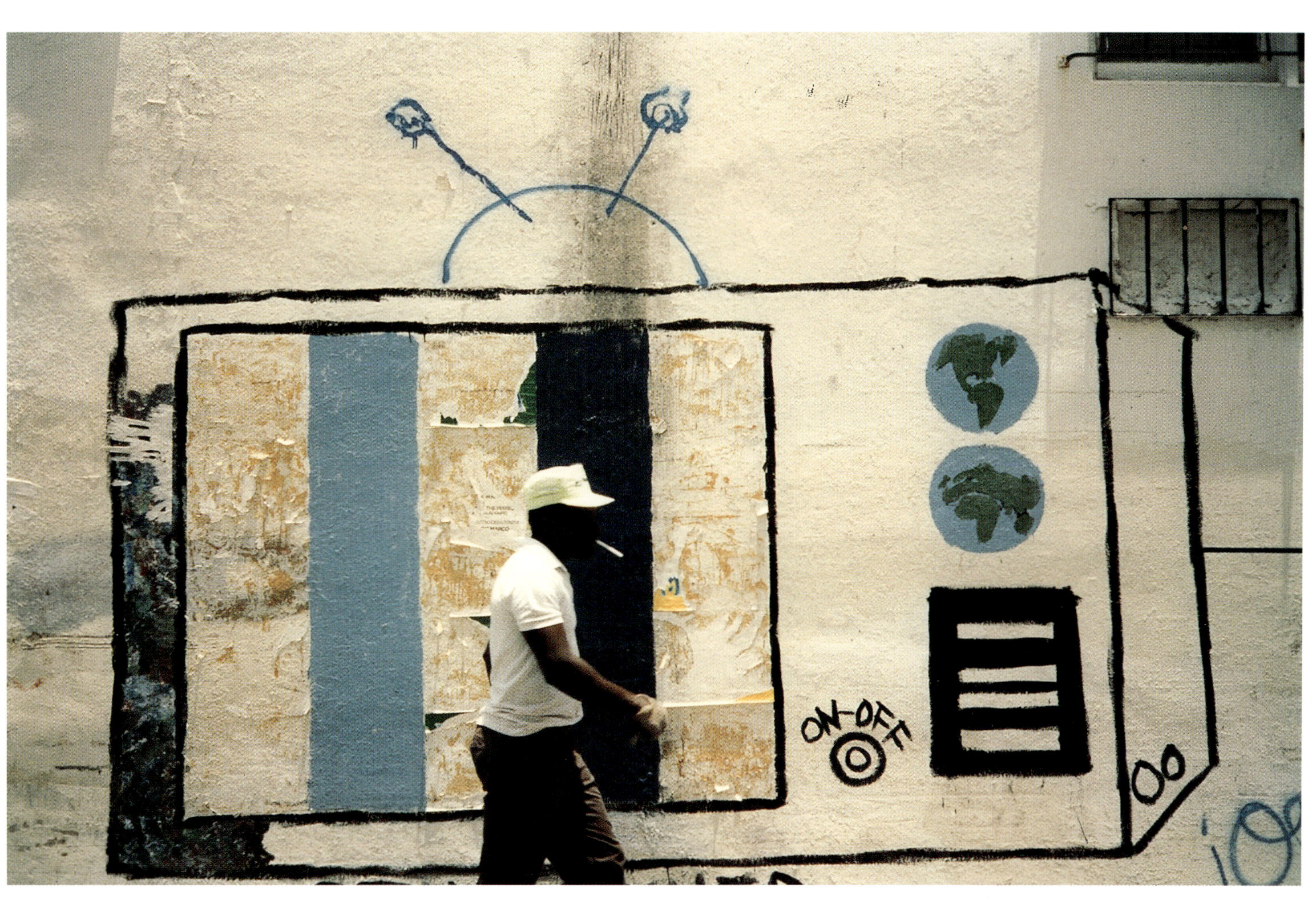

ON-OFF

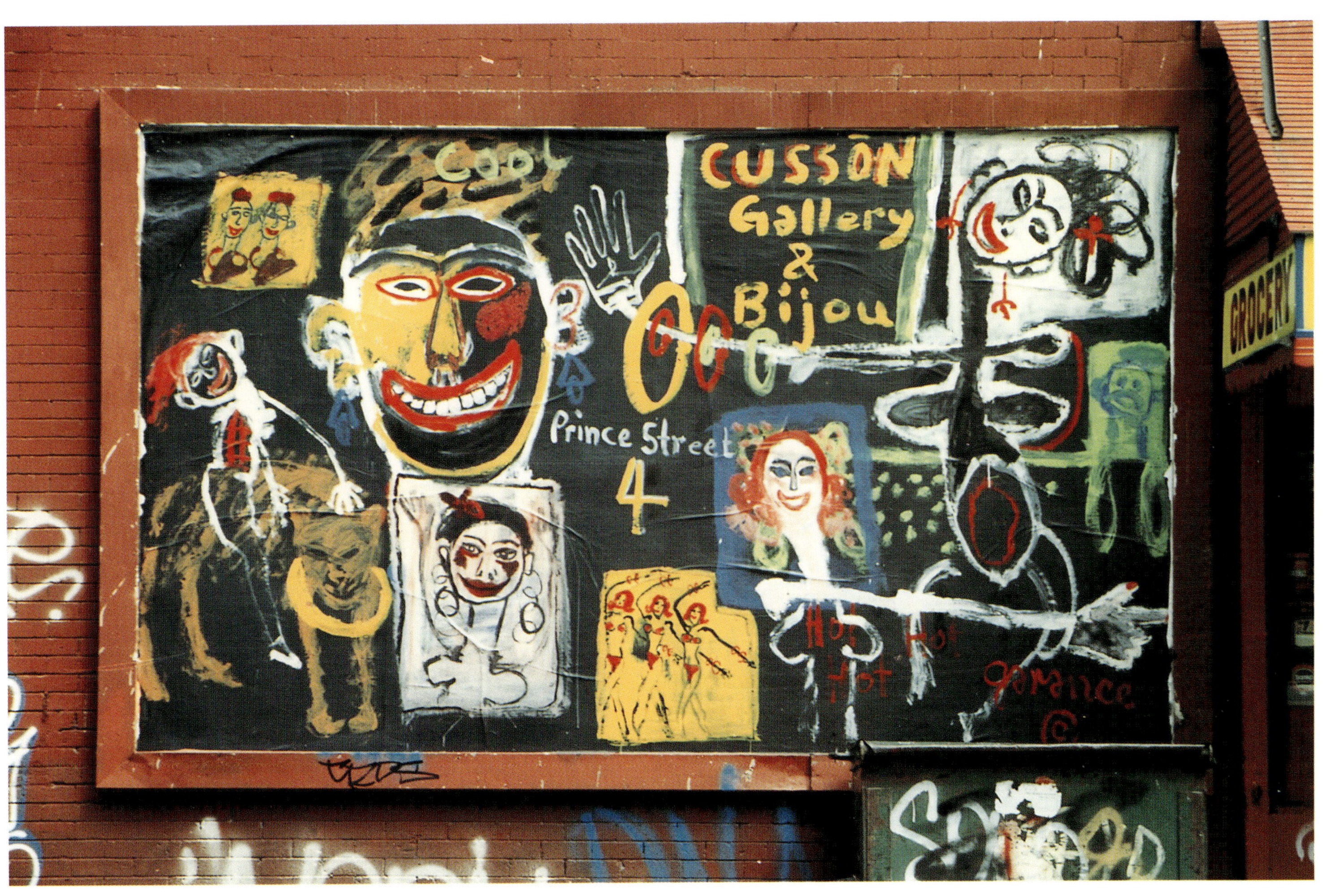
Cool
CUSSON
Gallery
&
Bijou
Prince Street
4
Hot
Hot
romance
GROCERY

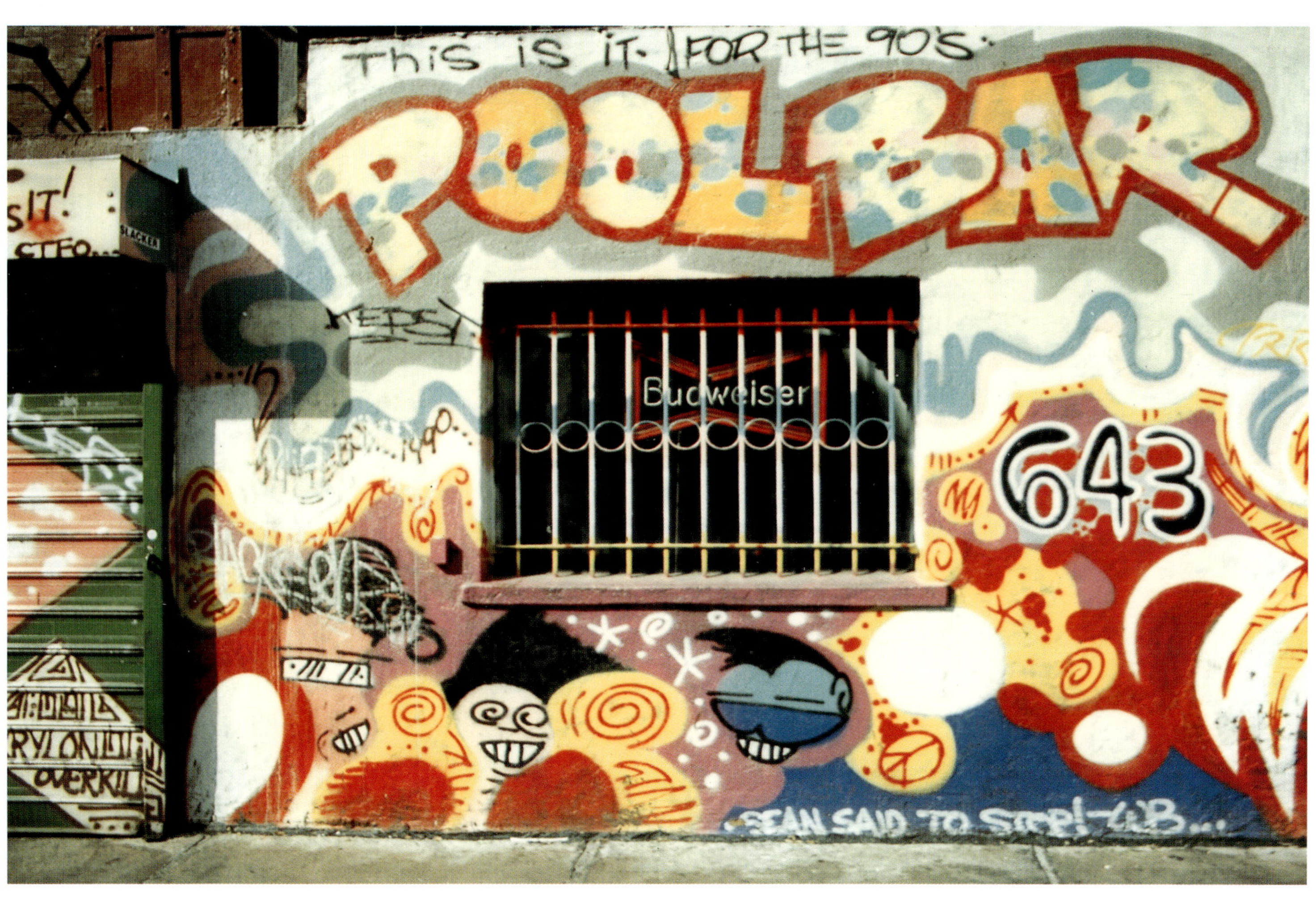

THIS IS IT. FOR THE 90'S
POOL BAR
Budweiser
643
SEAN SAID TO STOP! LB

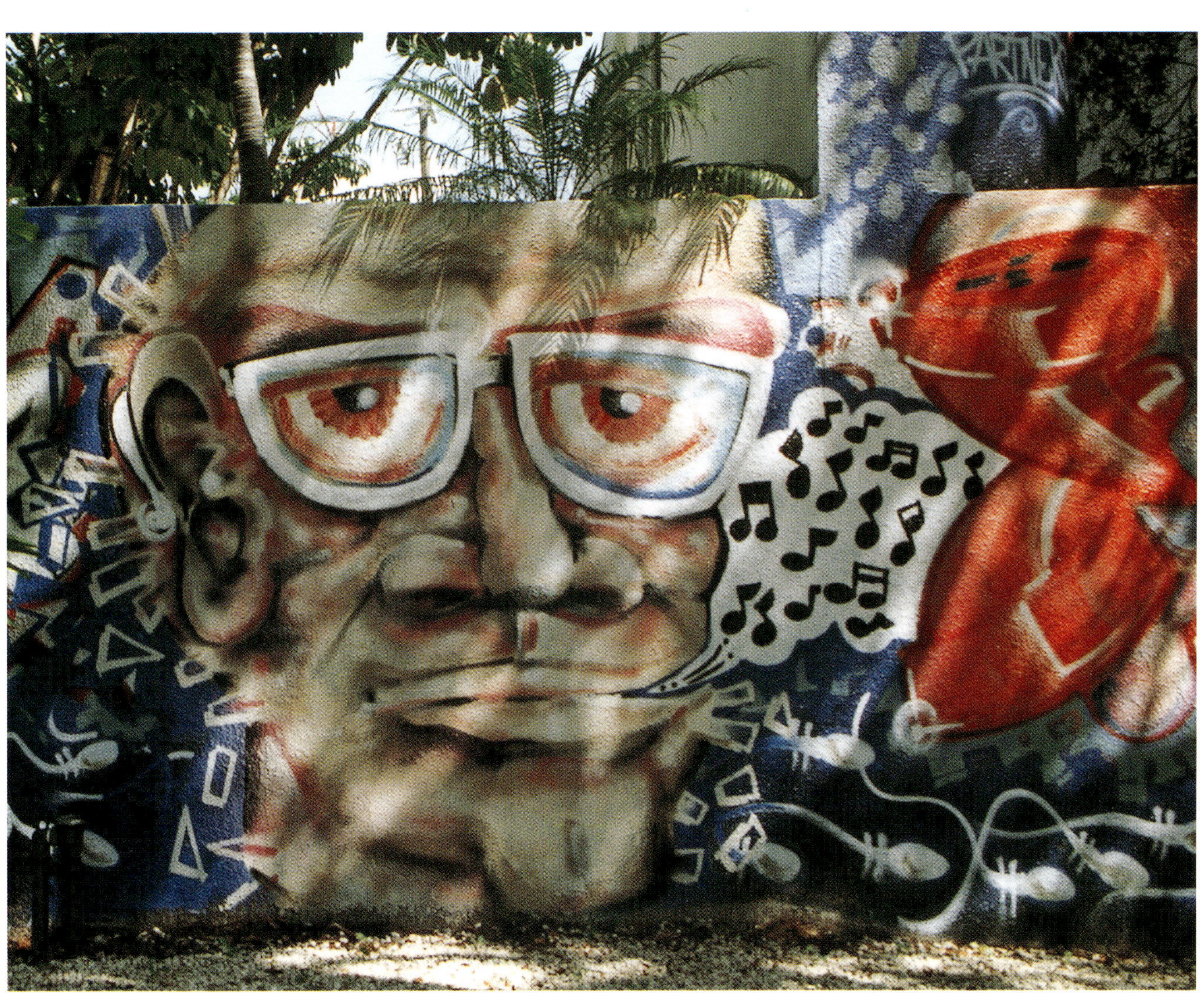

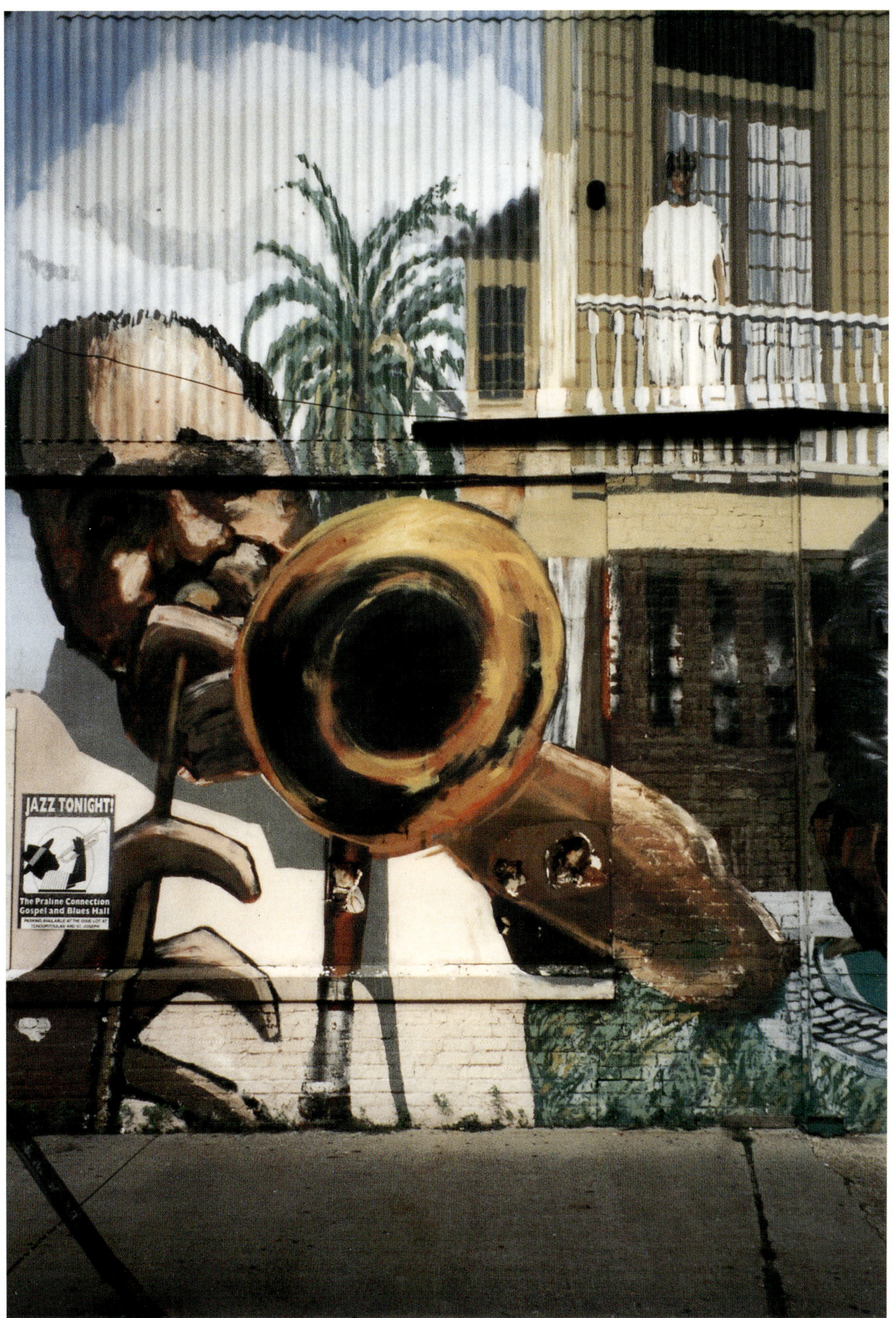

JAZZ TONIGHT!
The Praline Connection
Gospel and Blues Hall
PARKING AVAILABLE AT THE DIXIE LOT AT
TCHOUPITOULAS AND ST. JOSEPH

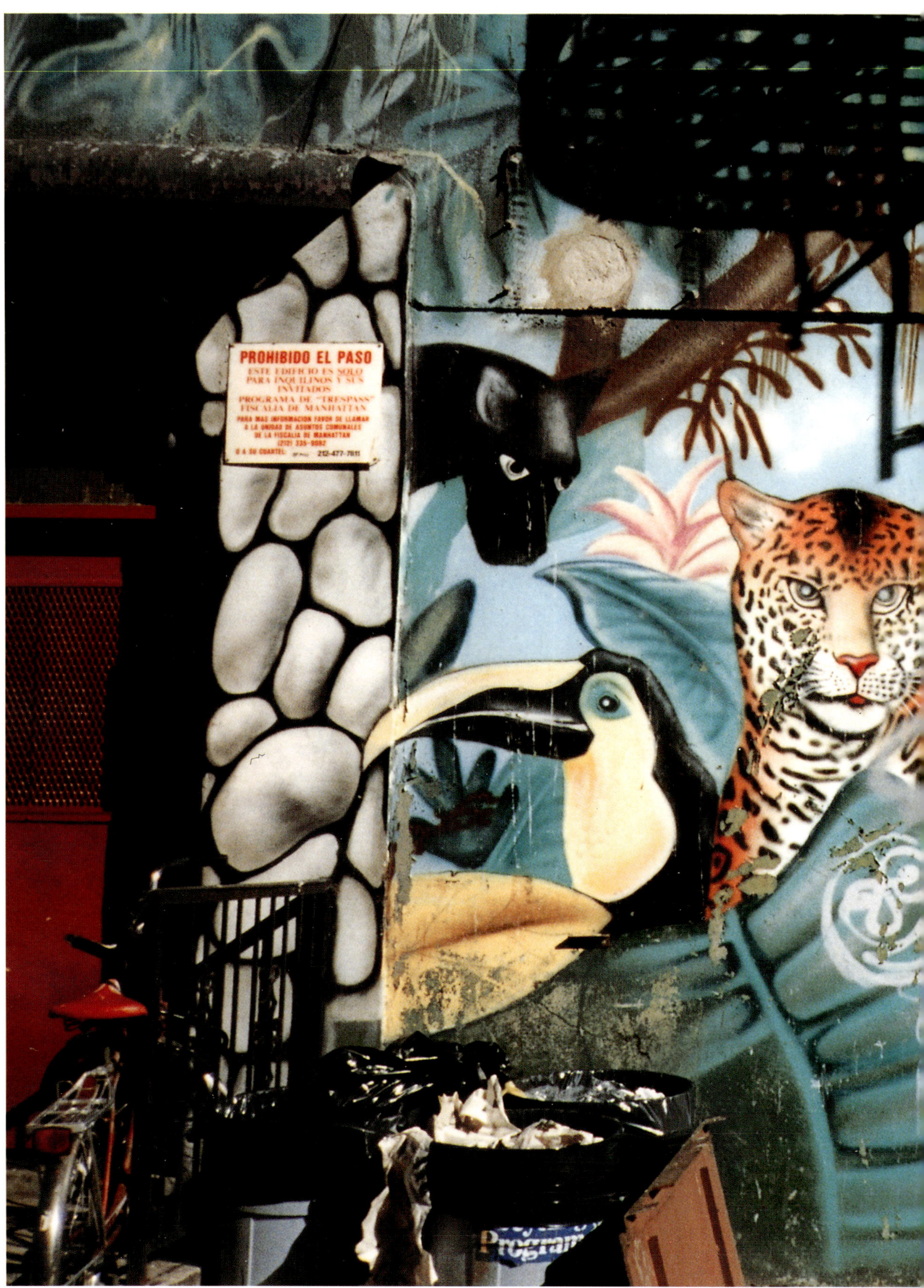
PROHIBIDO EL PASO
ESTE EDIFICIO ES SOLO
PARA INQUILINOS Y SUS
INVITADOS
PROGRAMA DE "TRESPASS"
FISCALIA DE MANHATTAN
PARA MAS INFORMACION FAVOR DE LLAMAR
A LA UNIDAD DE ASUNTOS COMUNALES
DE LA FISCALIA DE MANHATTAN
(212) 335-9082
O A SU CUARTEL   212-477-7811

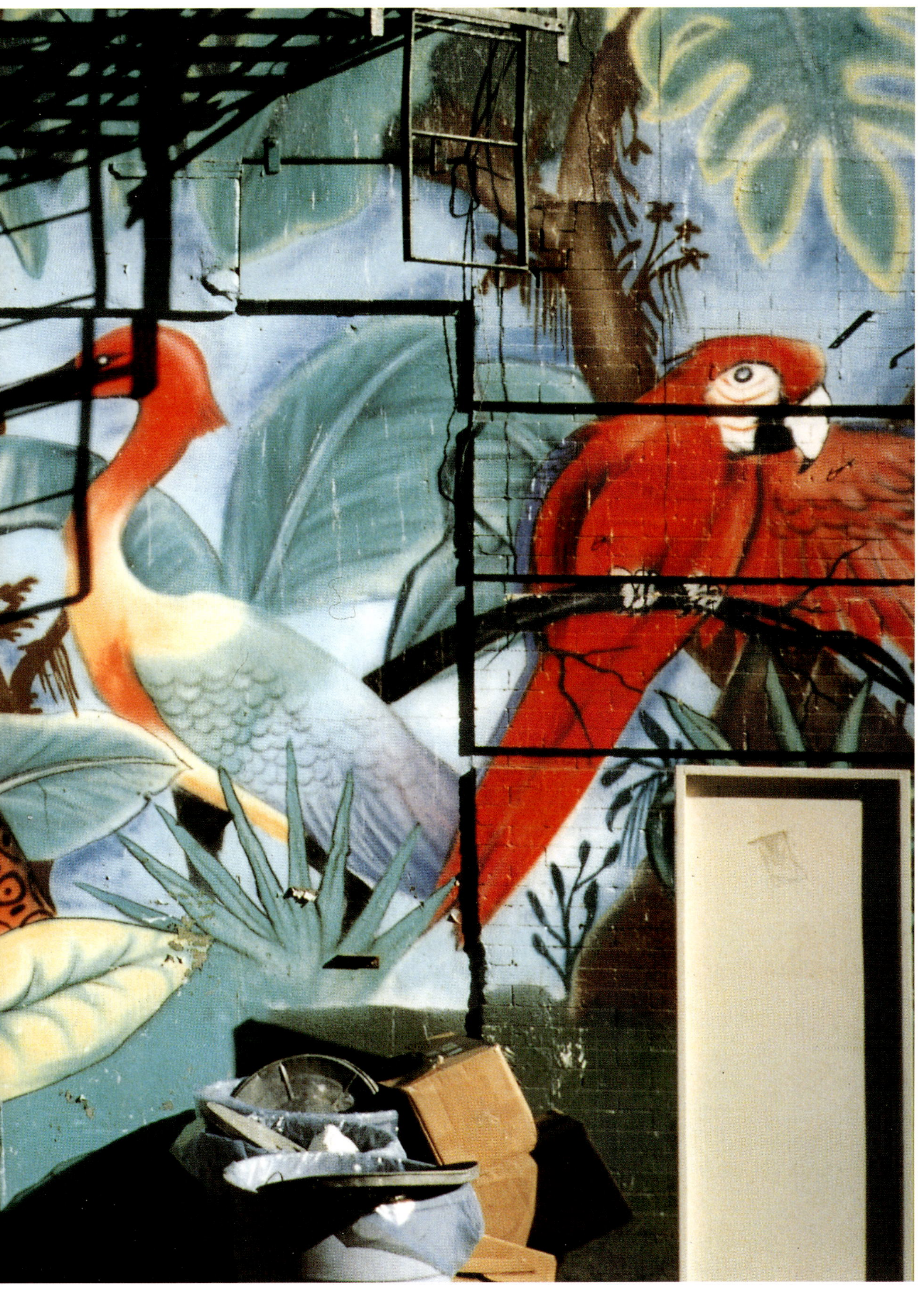

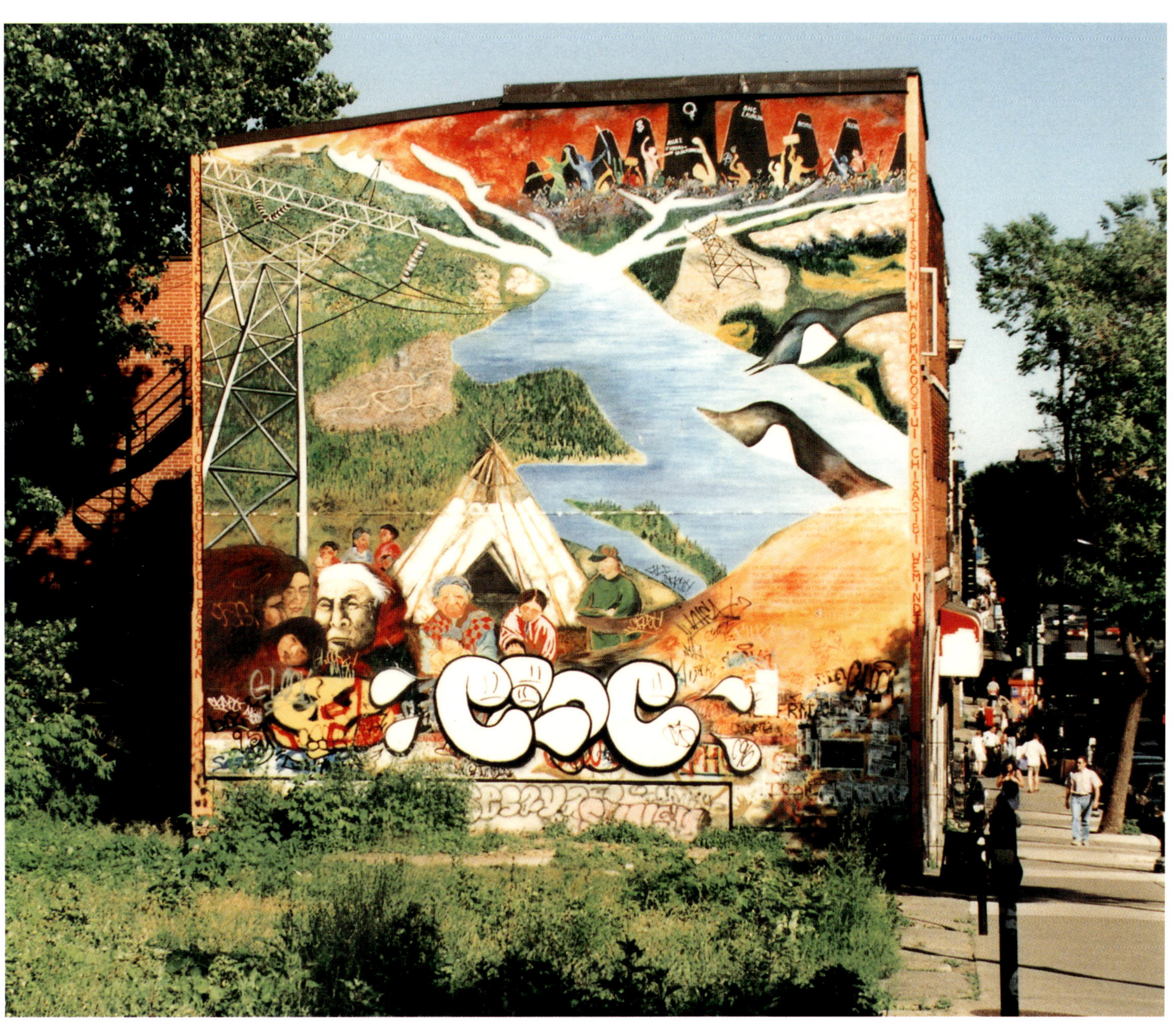

LAC MISTASSINI WHAPMAGOOSTUI CHISASIBI WEMINDJI

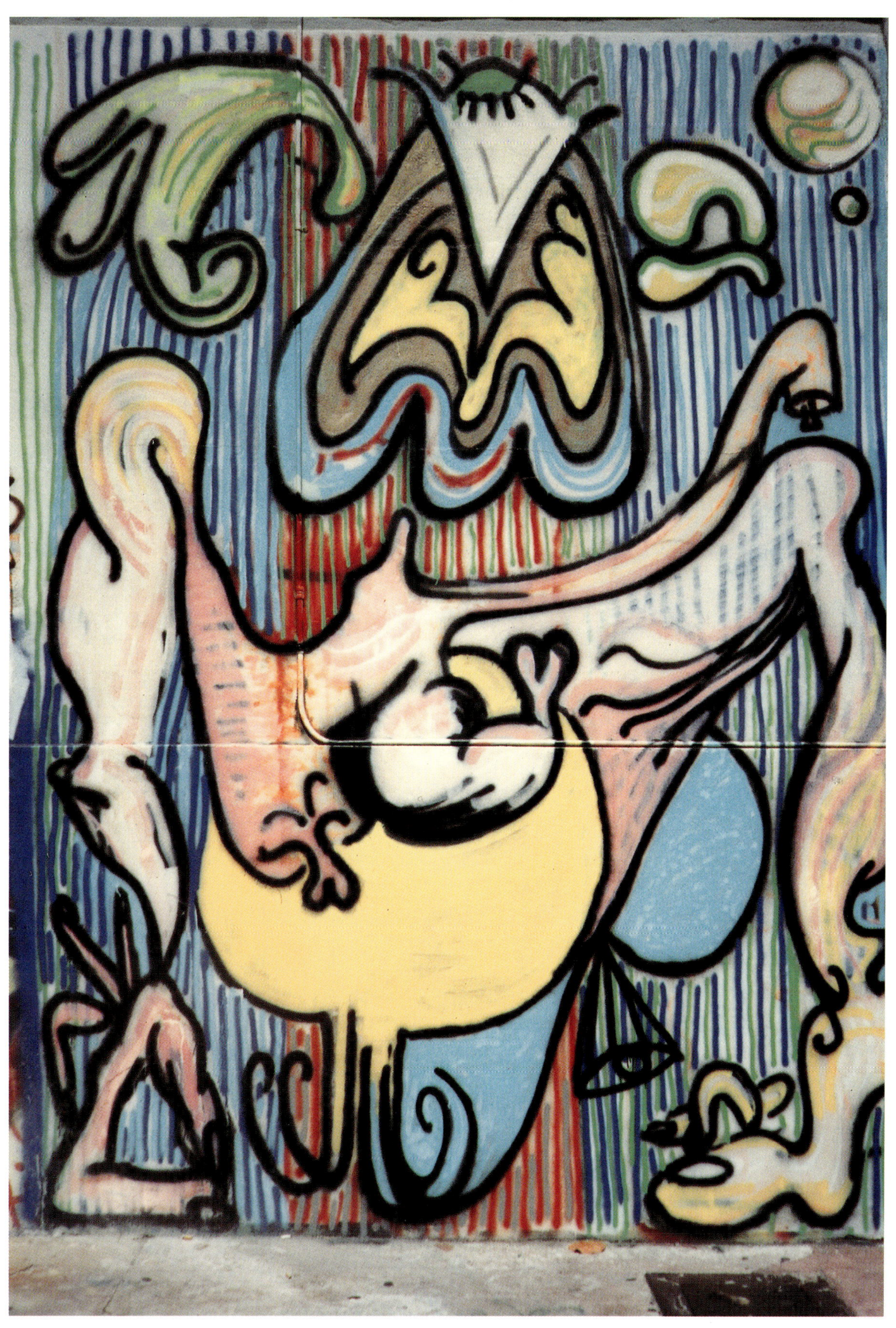

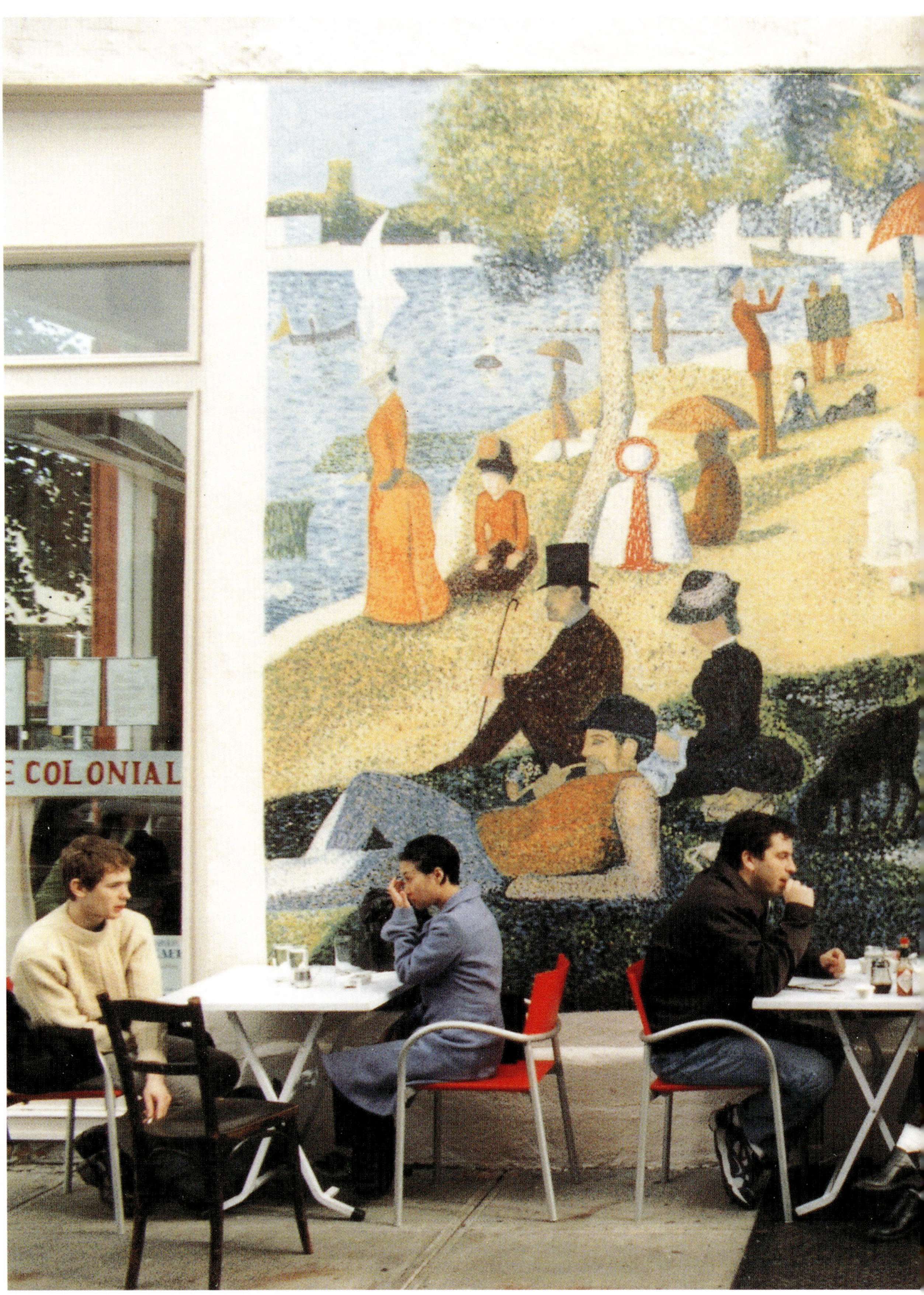

COLONIAL

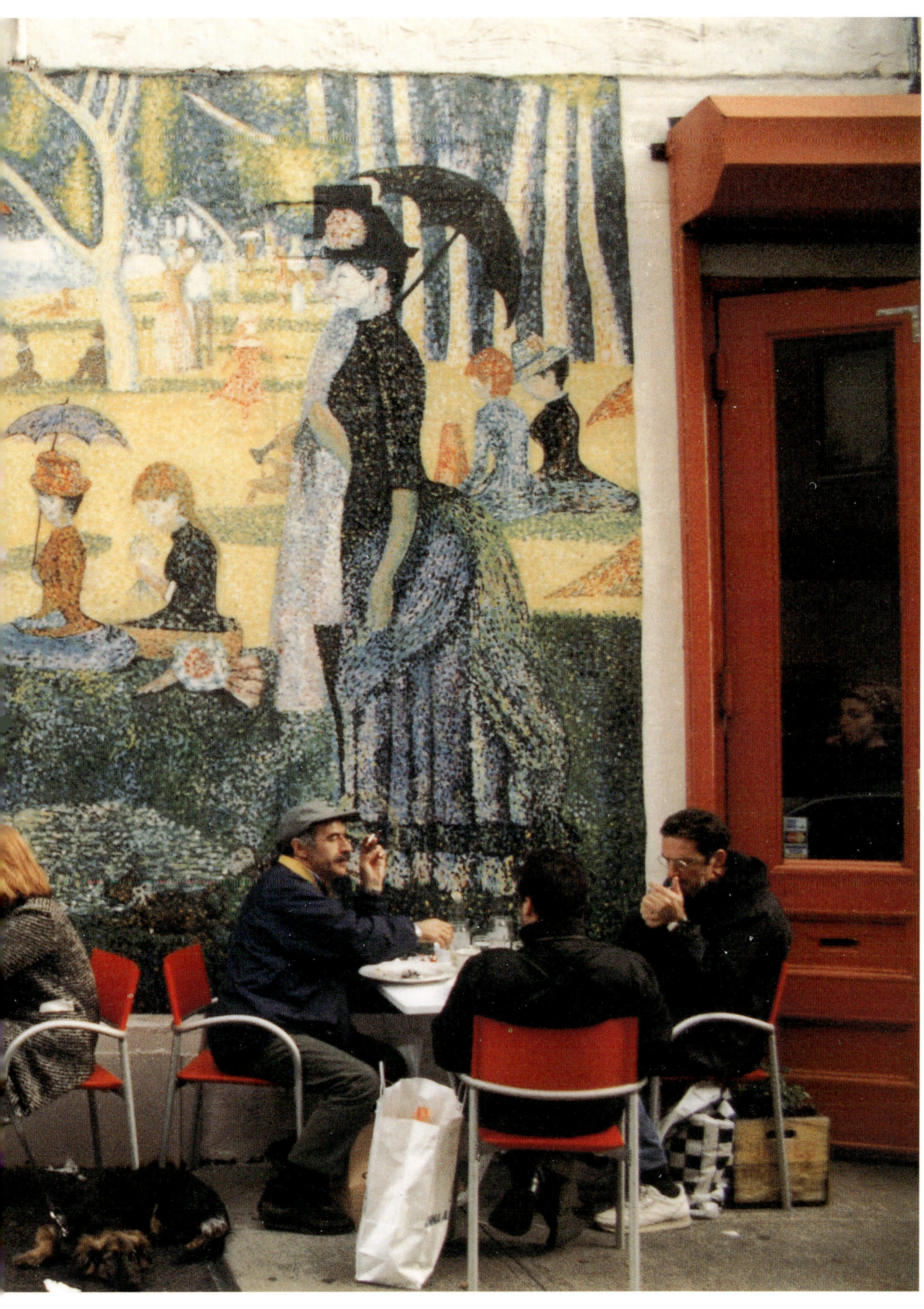

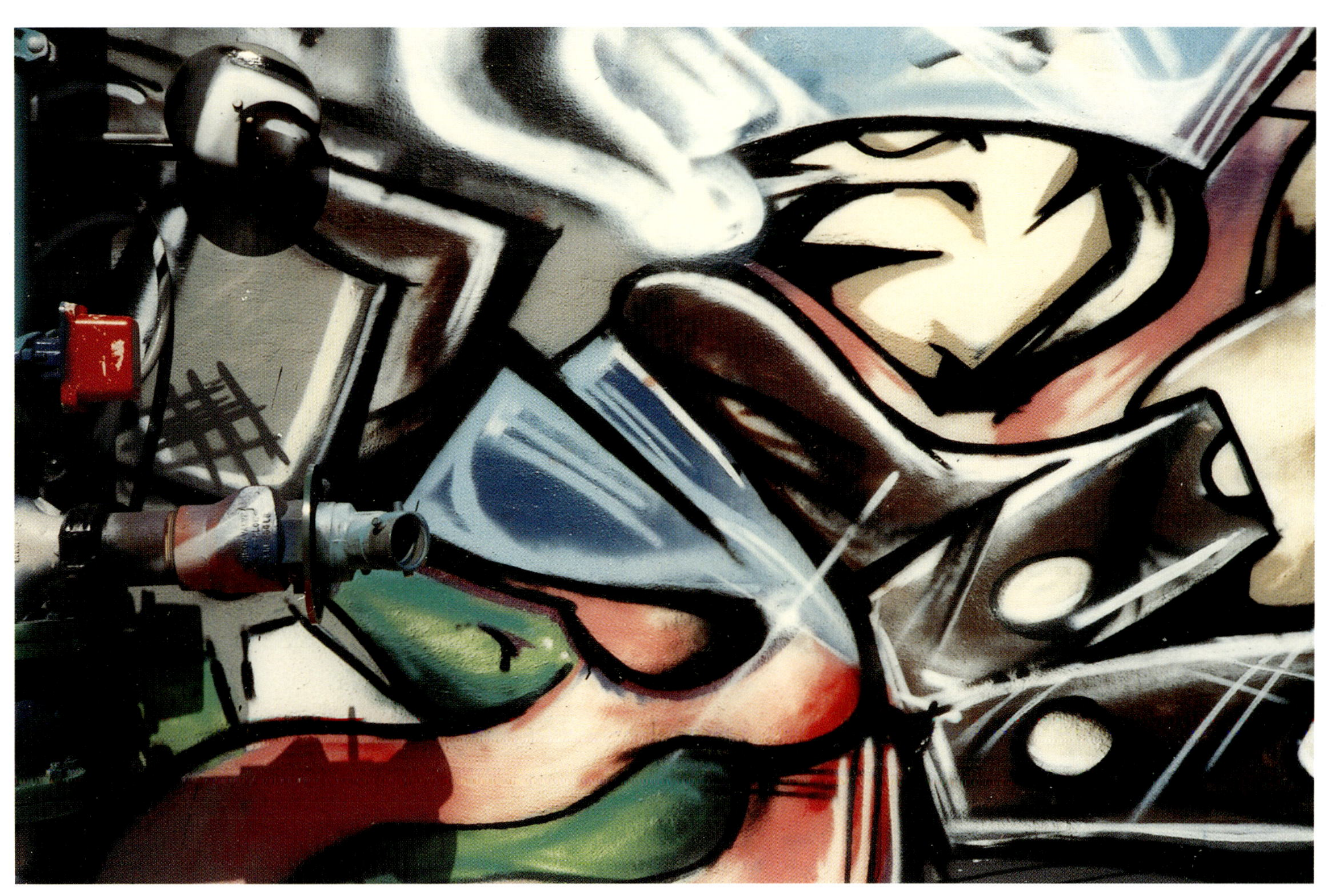

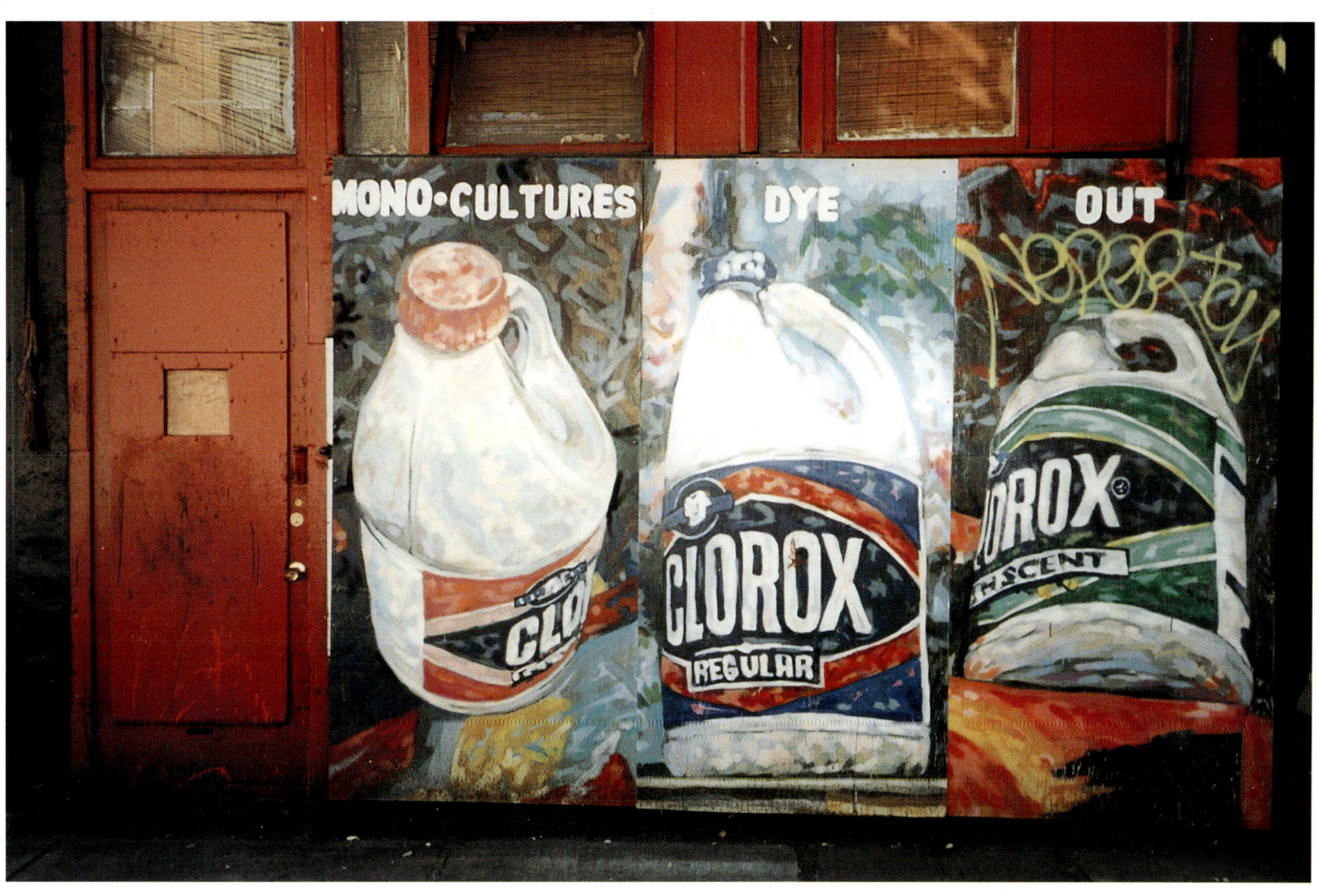

MONO·CULTURES
DYE
OUT
CLOROX
CLOROX
REGULAR
LOROX
SCENT

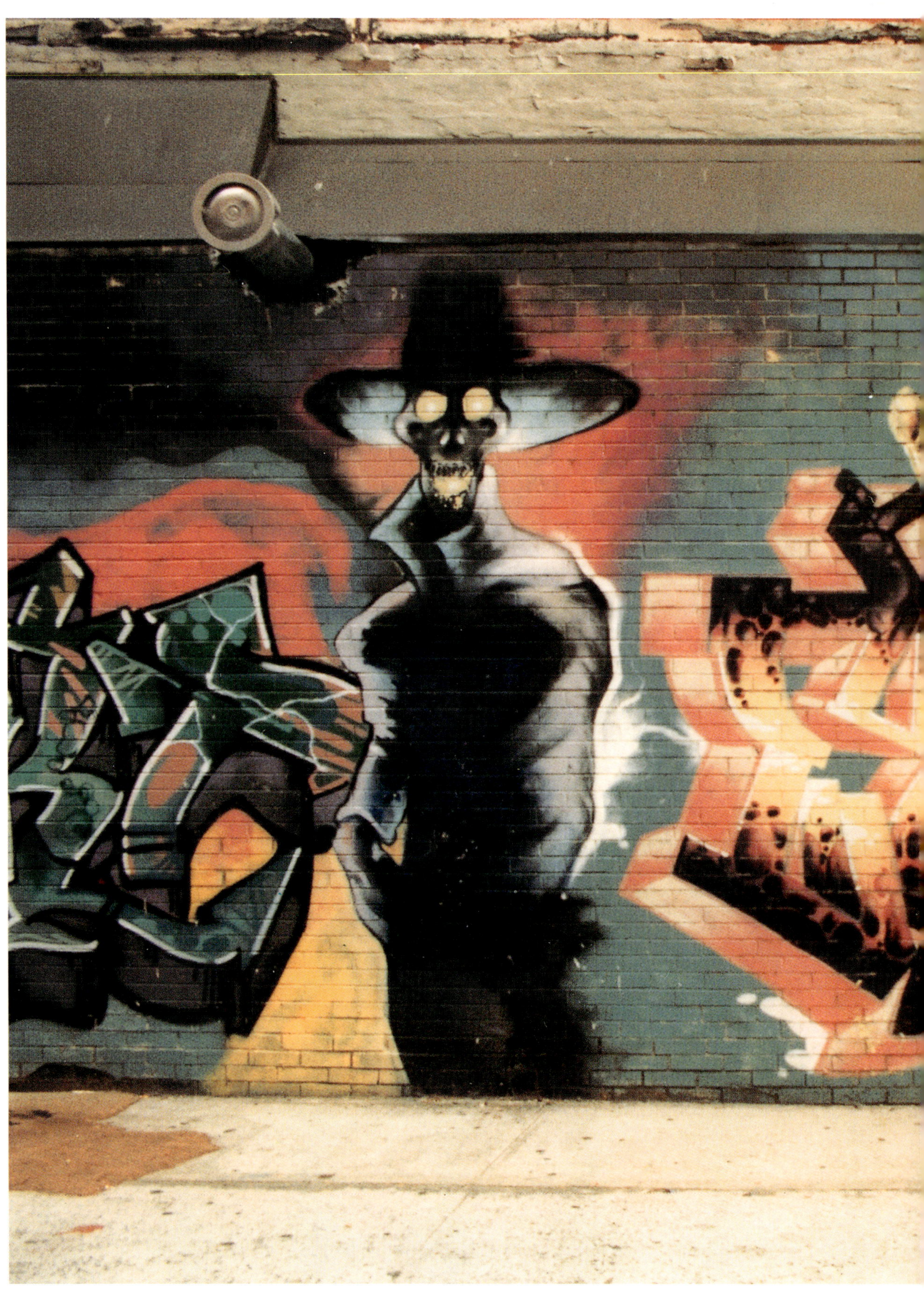

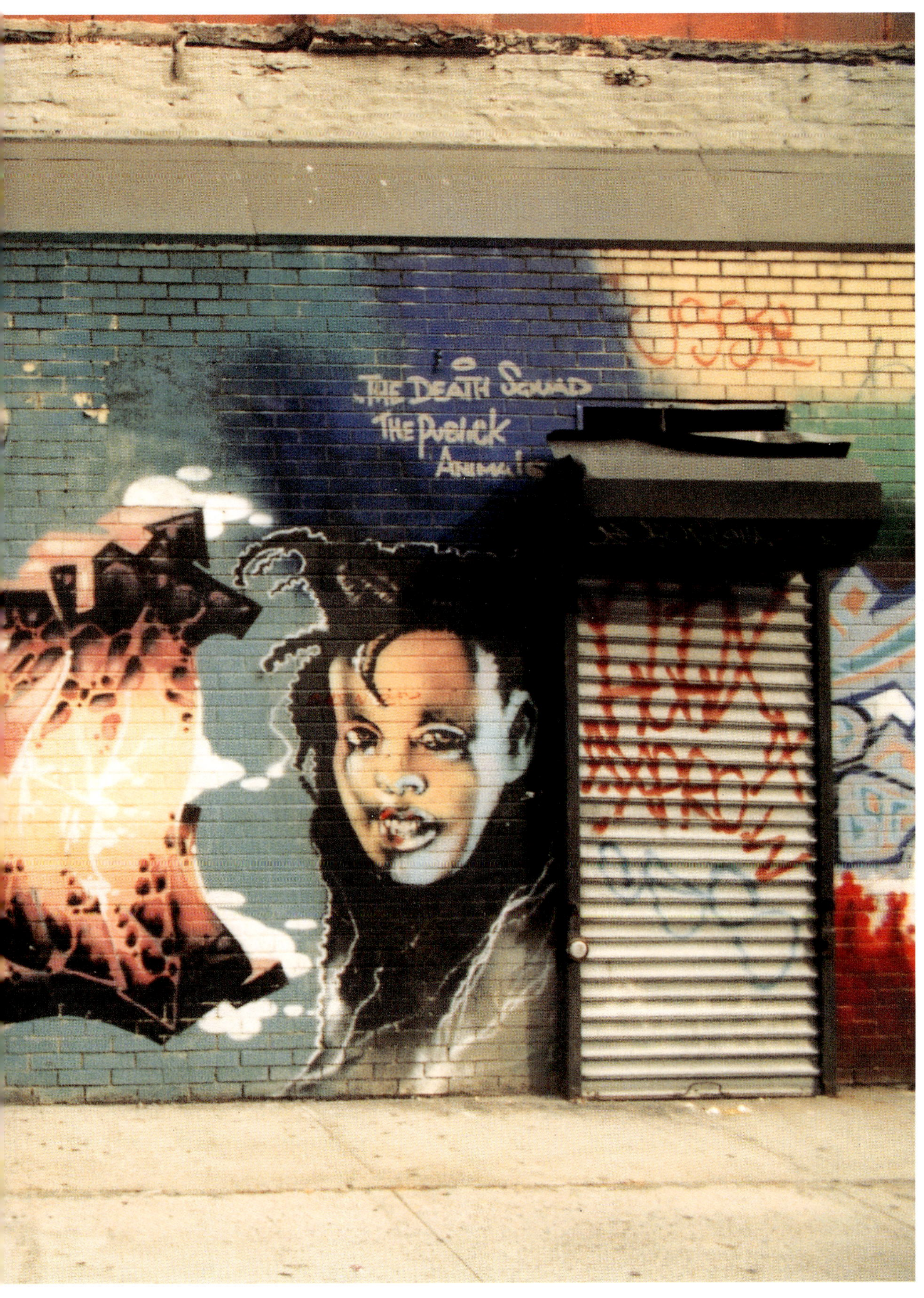

THE DEATH SQUAD
THE PUBLICK
ANIMALS

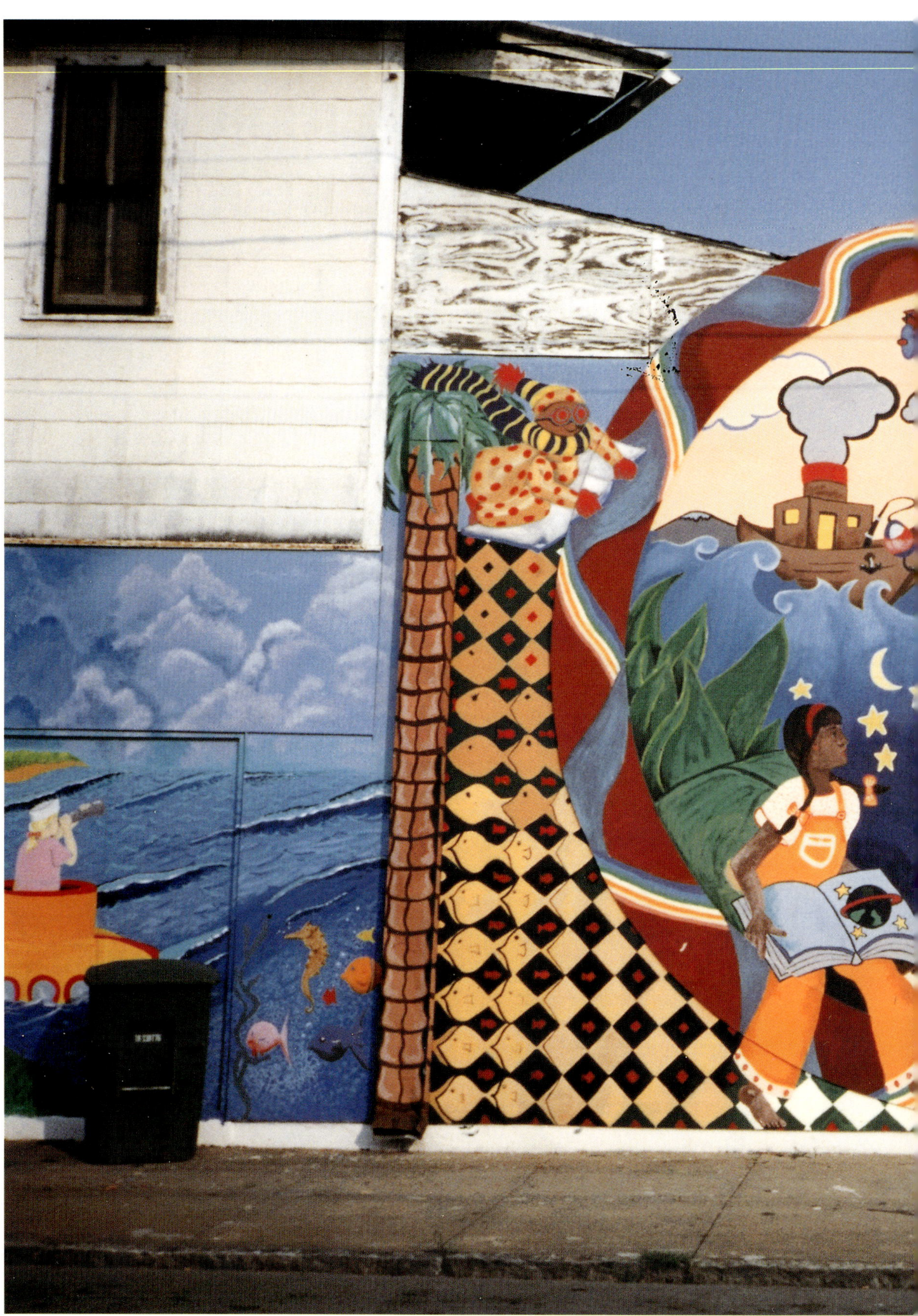

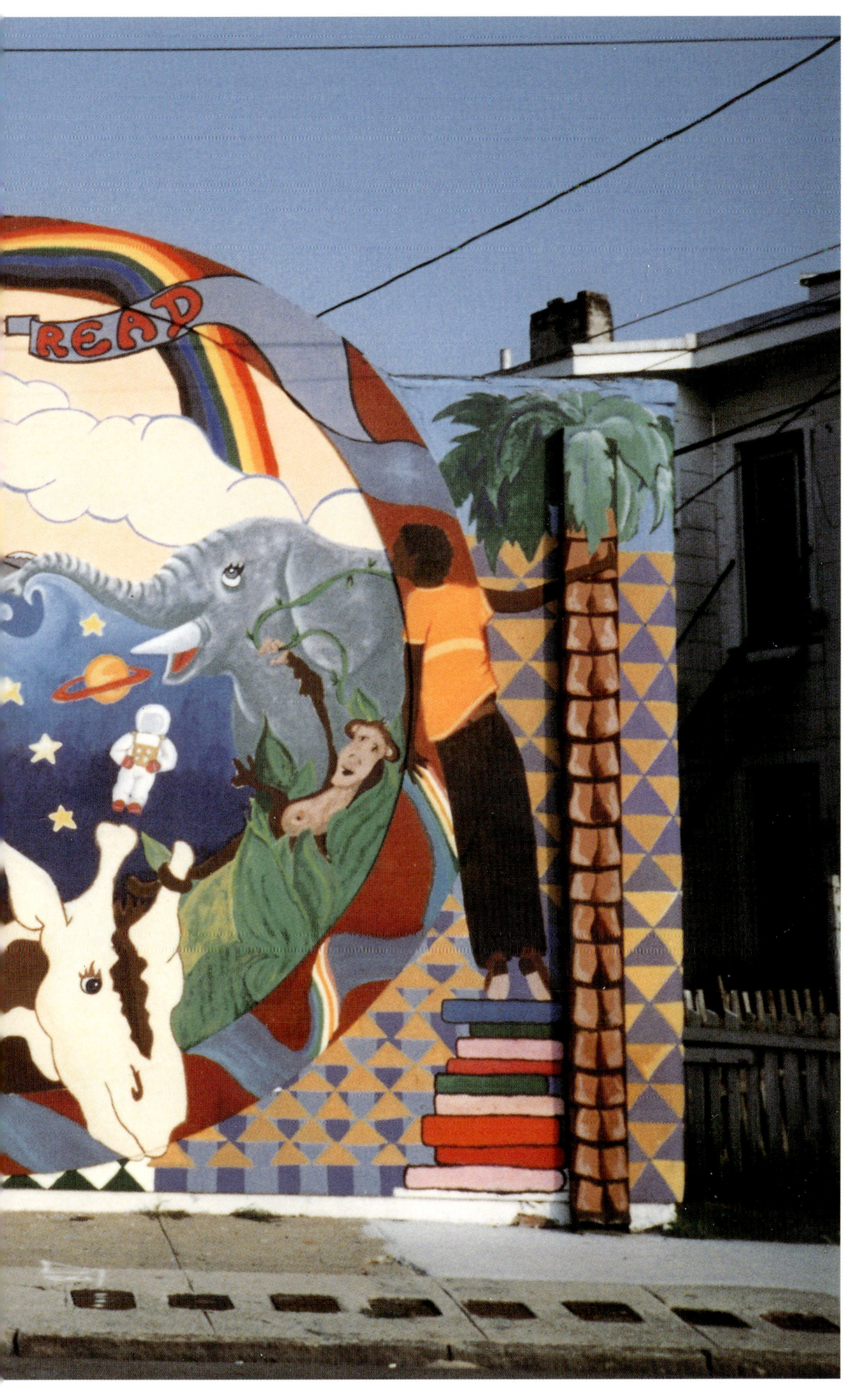
READ

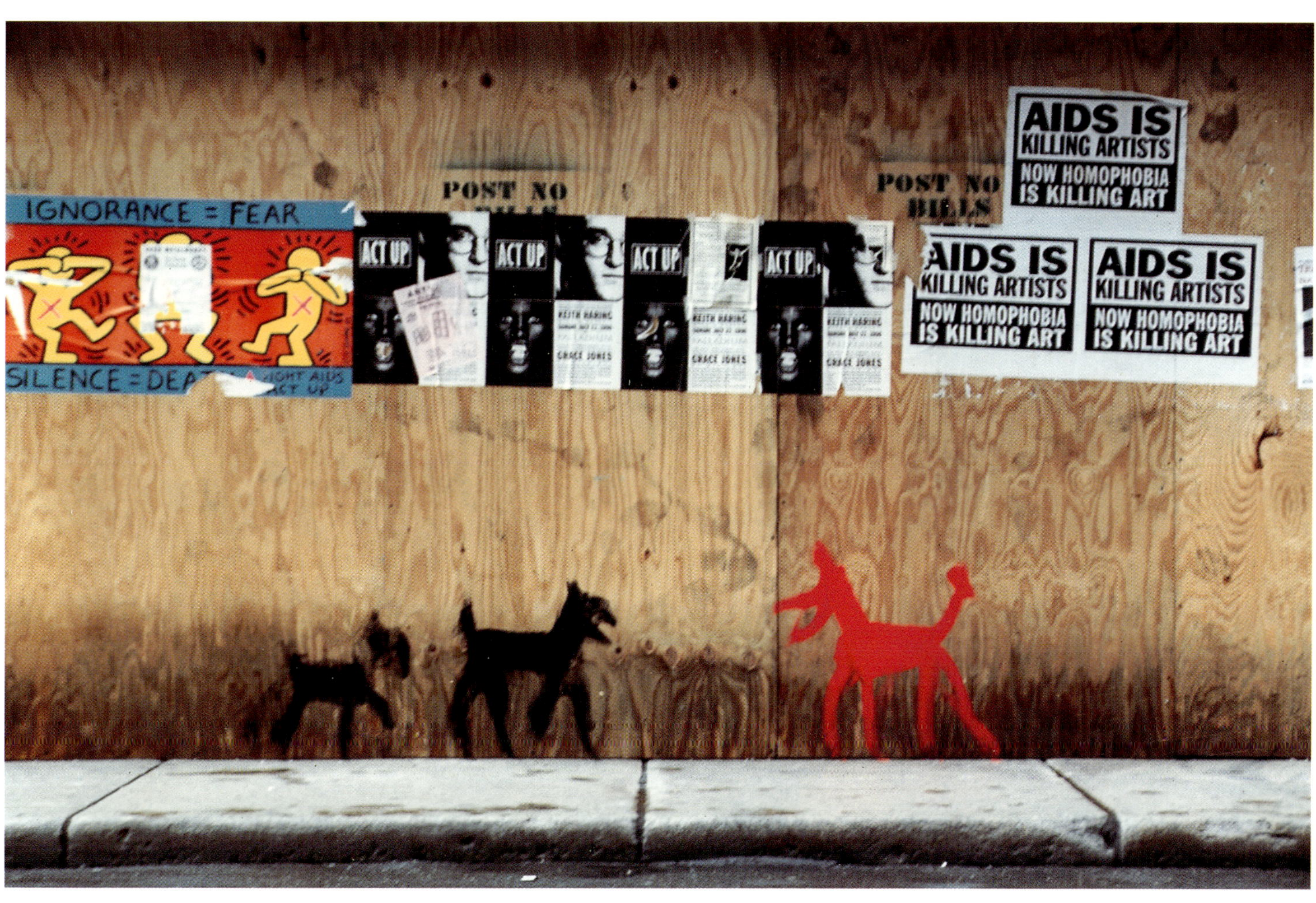

IGNORANCE = FEAR
SILENCE = DEATH
FIGHT AIDS ACT UP
ACT UP
ACT UP
ACT UP
ACT UP
KEITH HARING
GRACE JONES
POST NO BILLS
POST NO BILLS
AIDS IS KILLING ARTISTS NOW HOMOPHOBIA IS KILLING ART
AIDS IS KILLING ARTISTS NOW HOMOPHOBIA IS KILLING ART
AIDS IS KILLING ARTISTS NOW HOMOPHOBIA IS KILLING ART

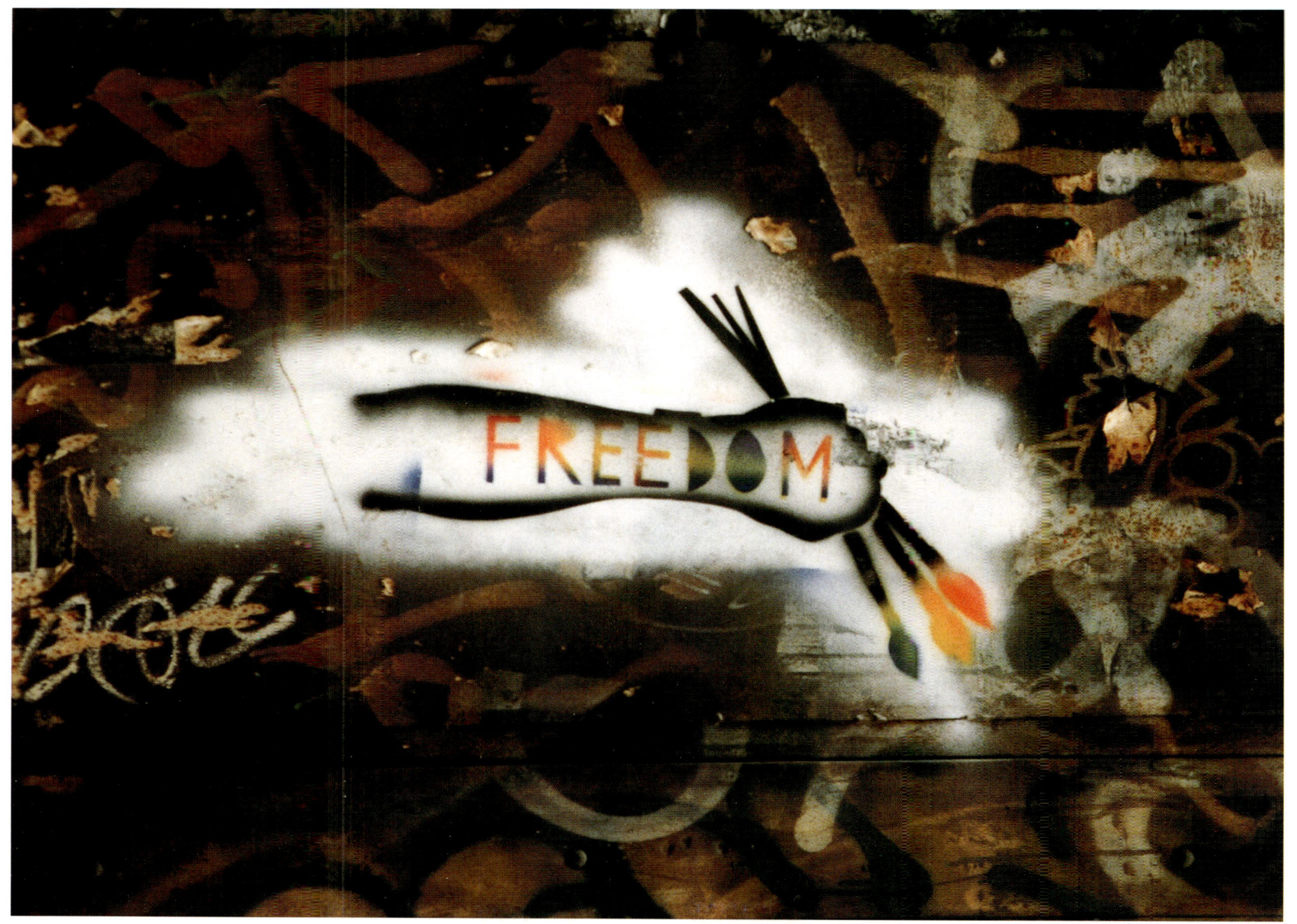
FREEDOM

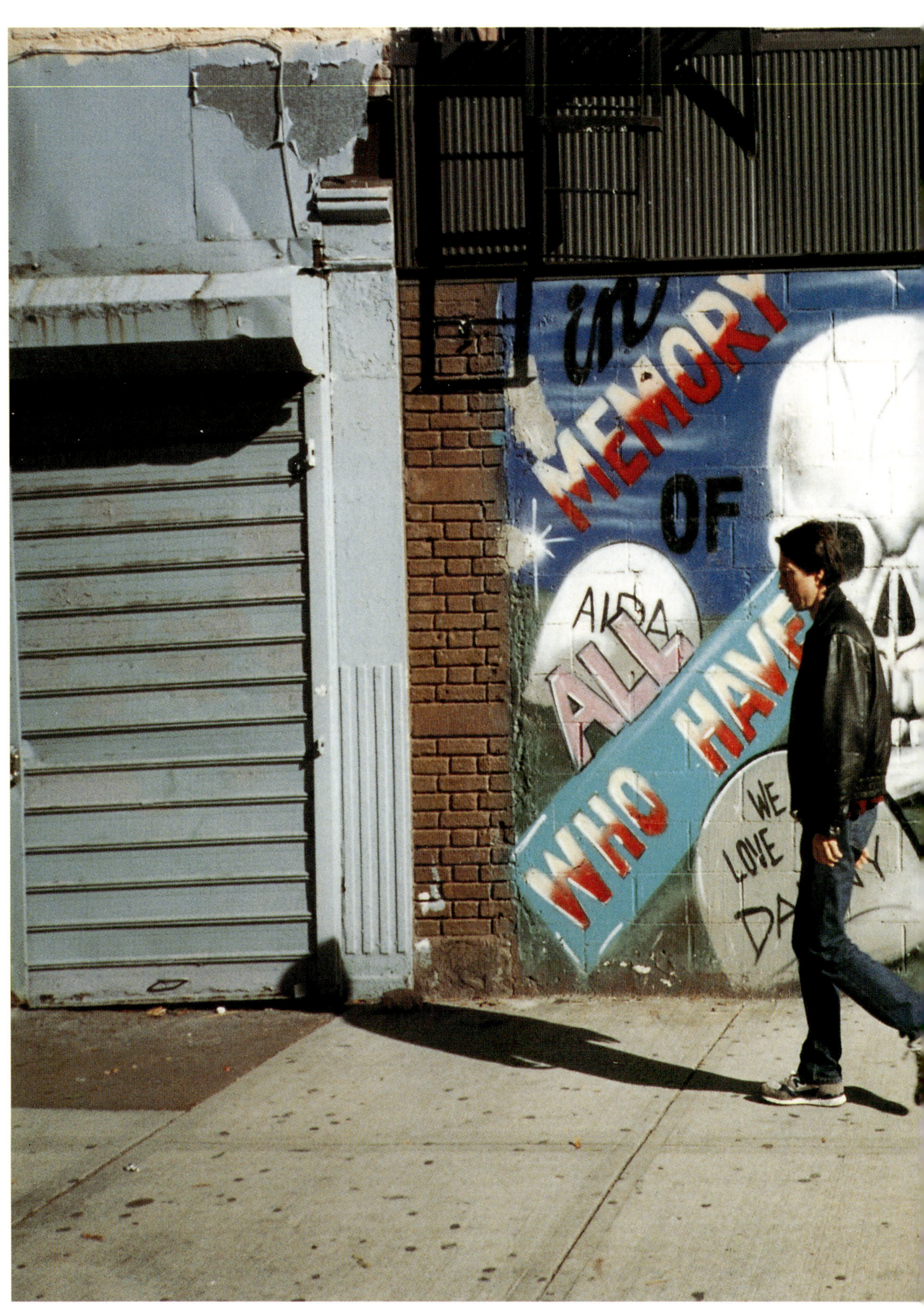
in
MEMORY
OF
ALL
WHO HAVE
AKA
WE
LOVE
DANNY

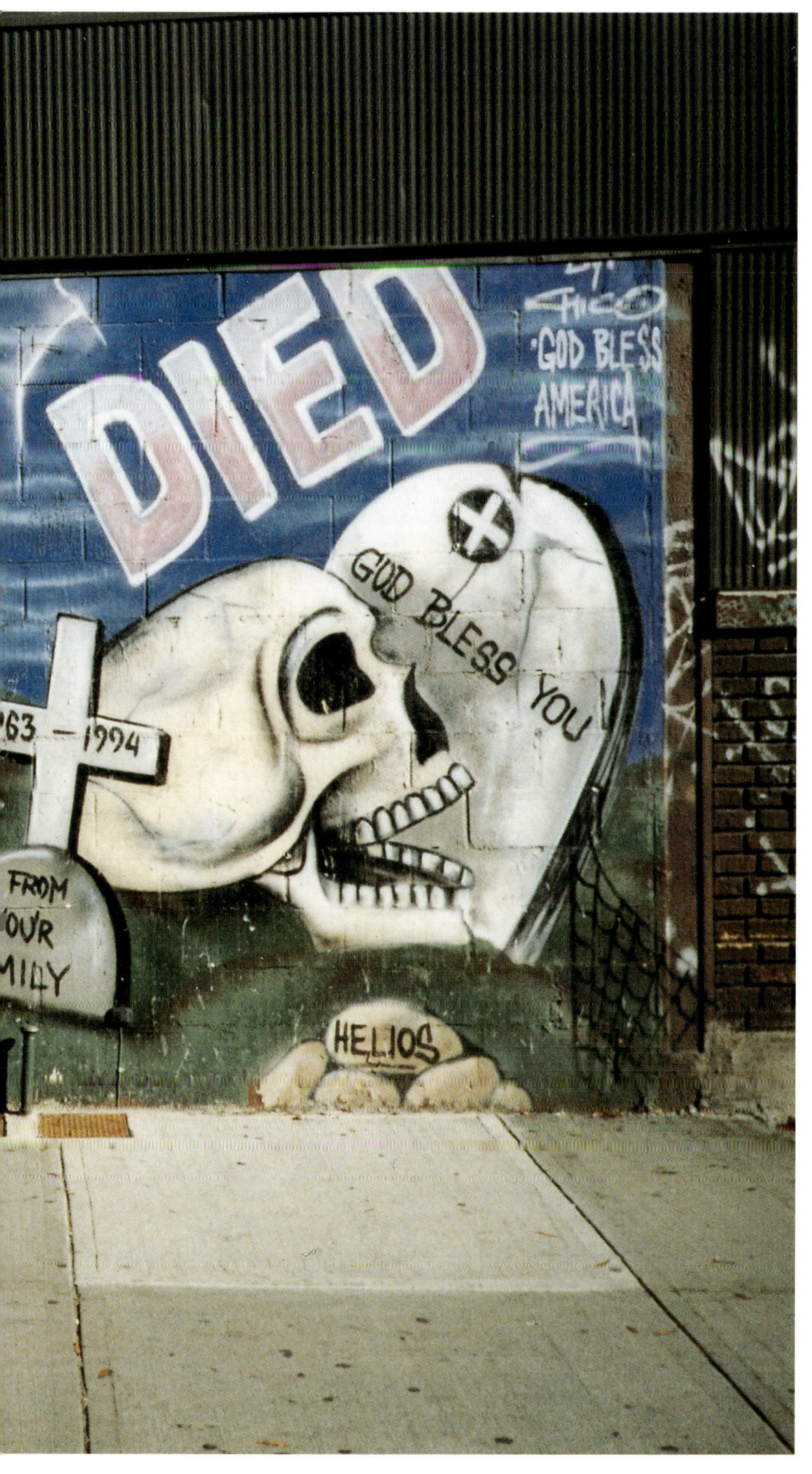

DIED
"GOD BLESS AMERICA
GOD BLESS YOU
63 - 1994
FROM OUR MIDY
HELIOS

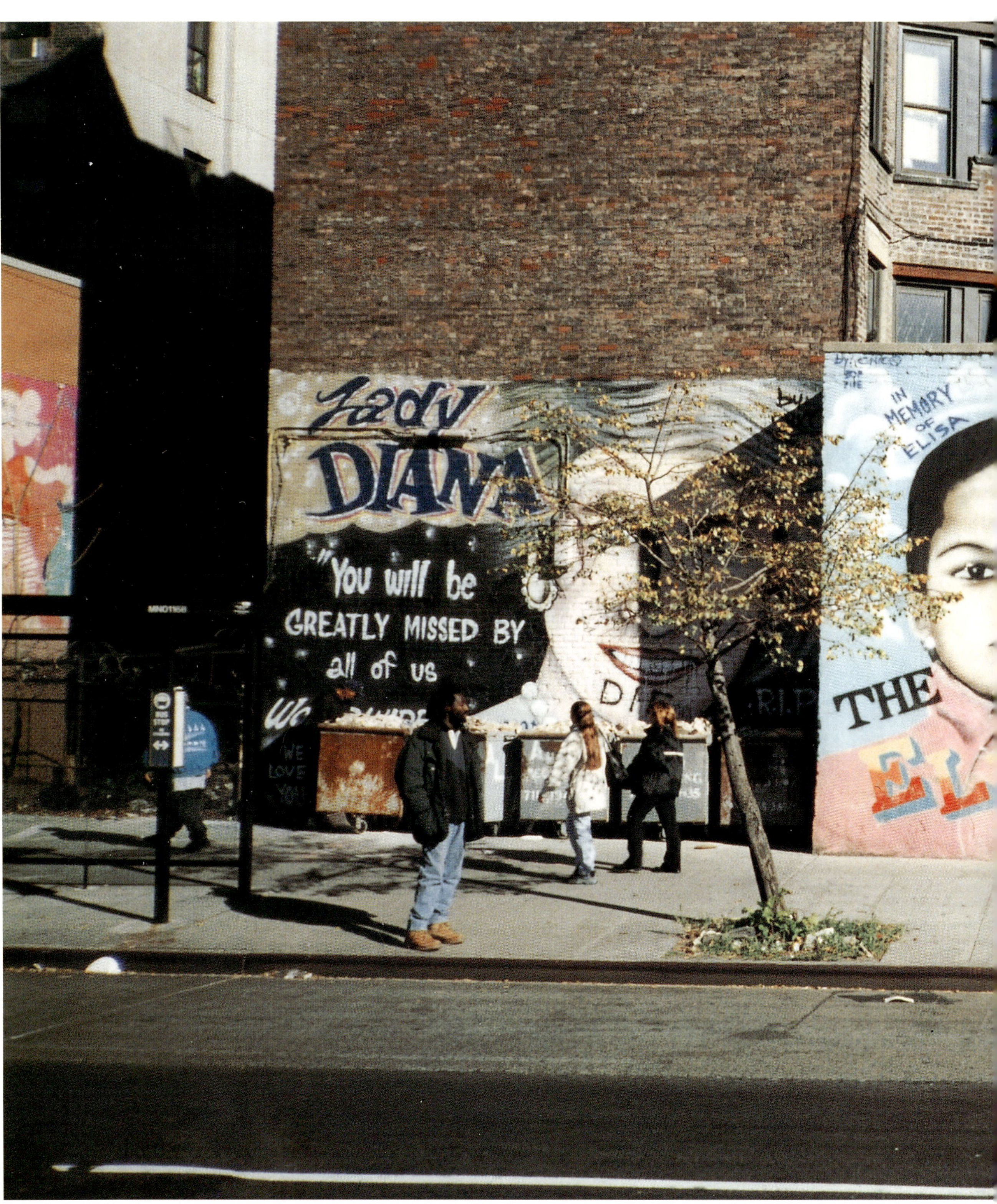
Lady
DIANA
"You will be
GREATLY MISSED BY
all of us
We
WE
LOVE
YOU!
R.I.P.
IN
MEMORY
OF
ELISA
THE
EL

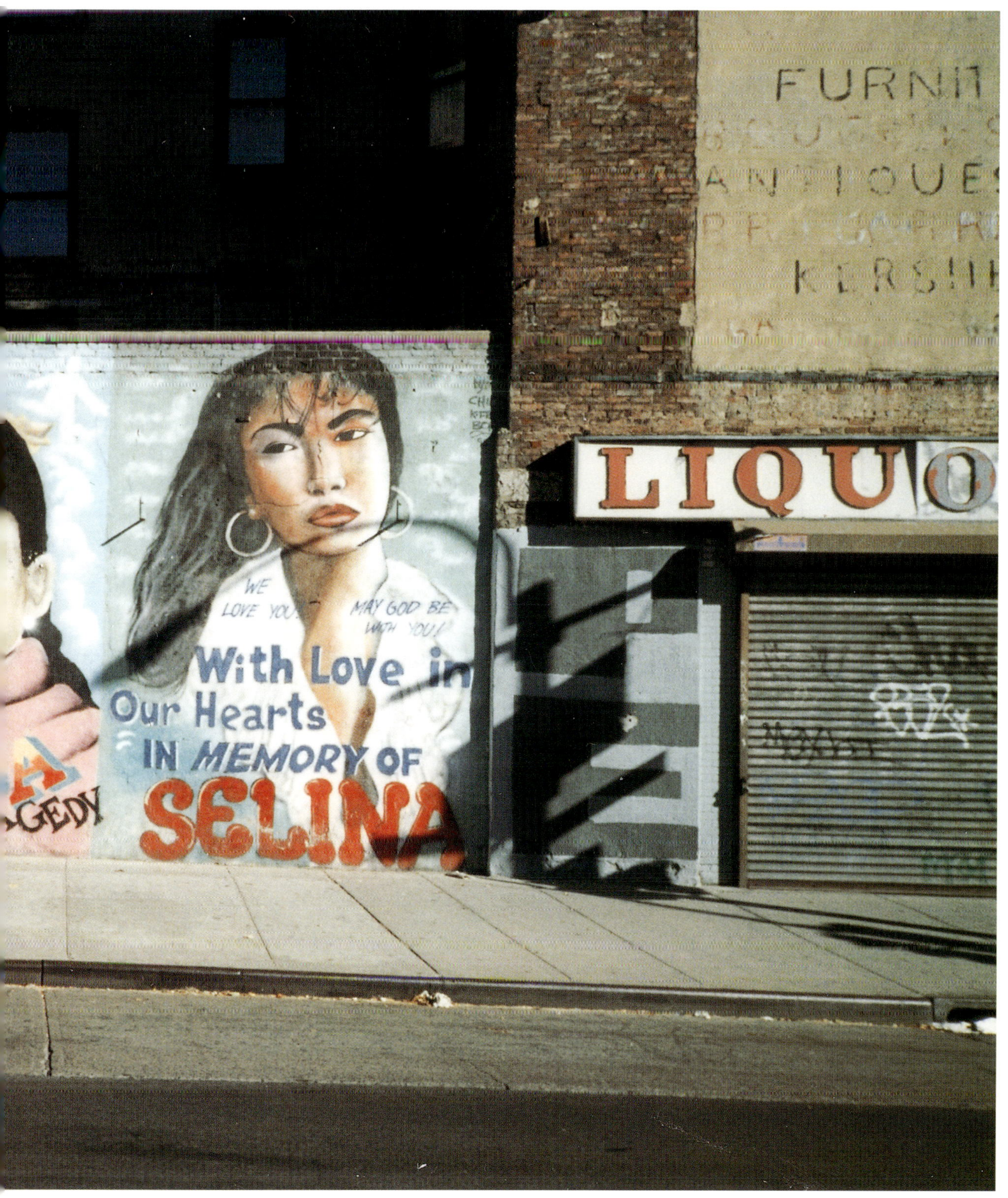

FURNIT
ANTIQUES
KERSH
LIQUO
WE
LOVE YOU!
MAY GOD BE
WITH YOU!
With Love in
Our Hearts
IN MEMORY OF
SELINA
GEDY

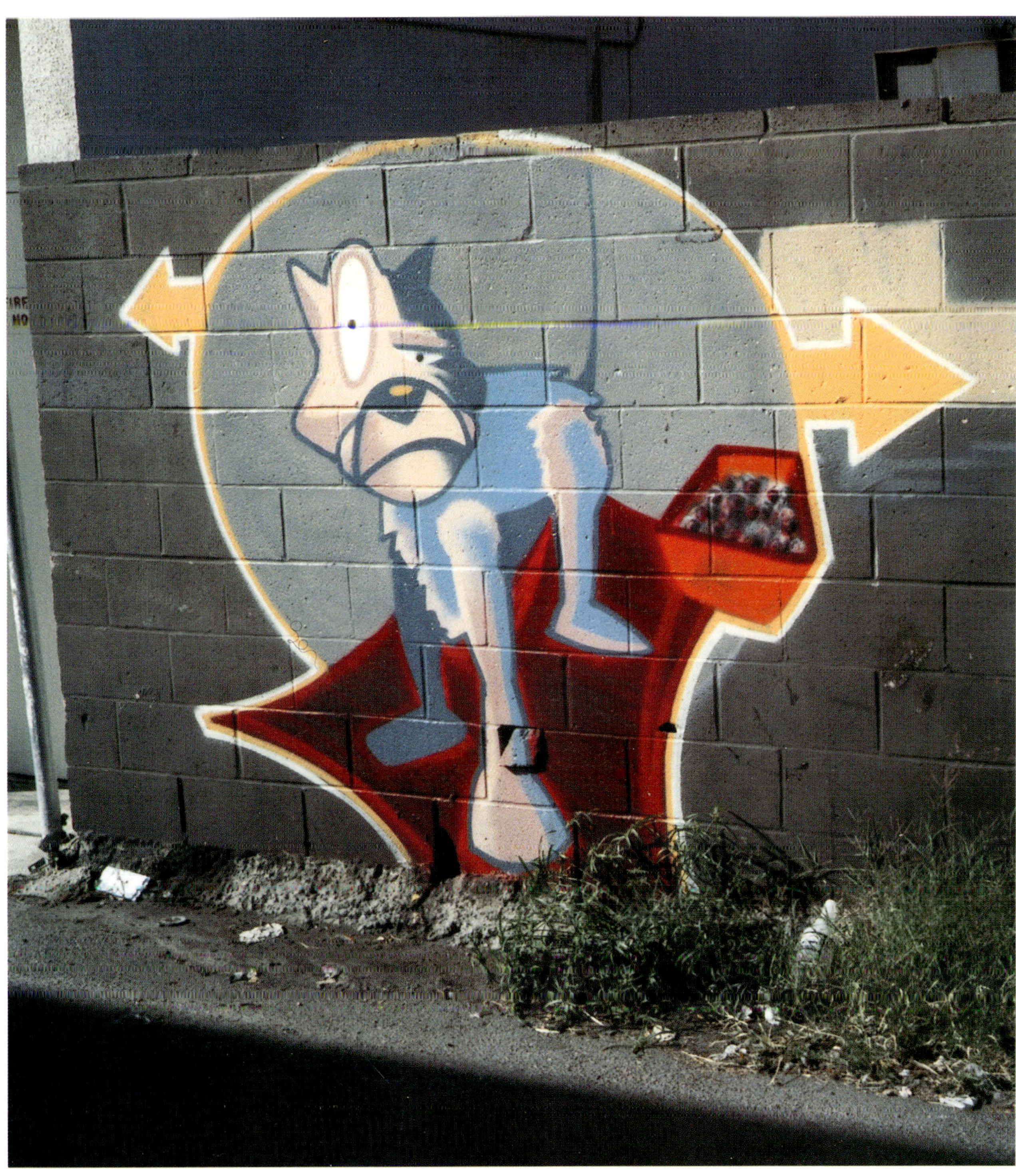

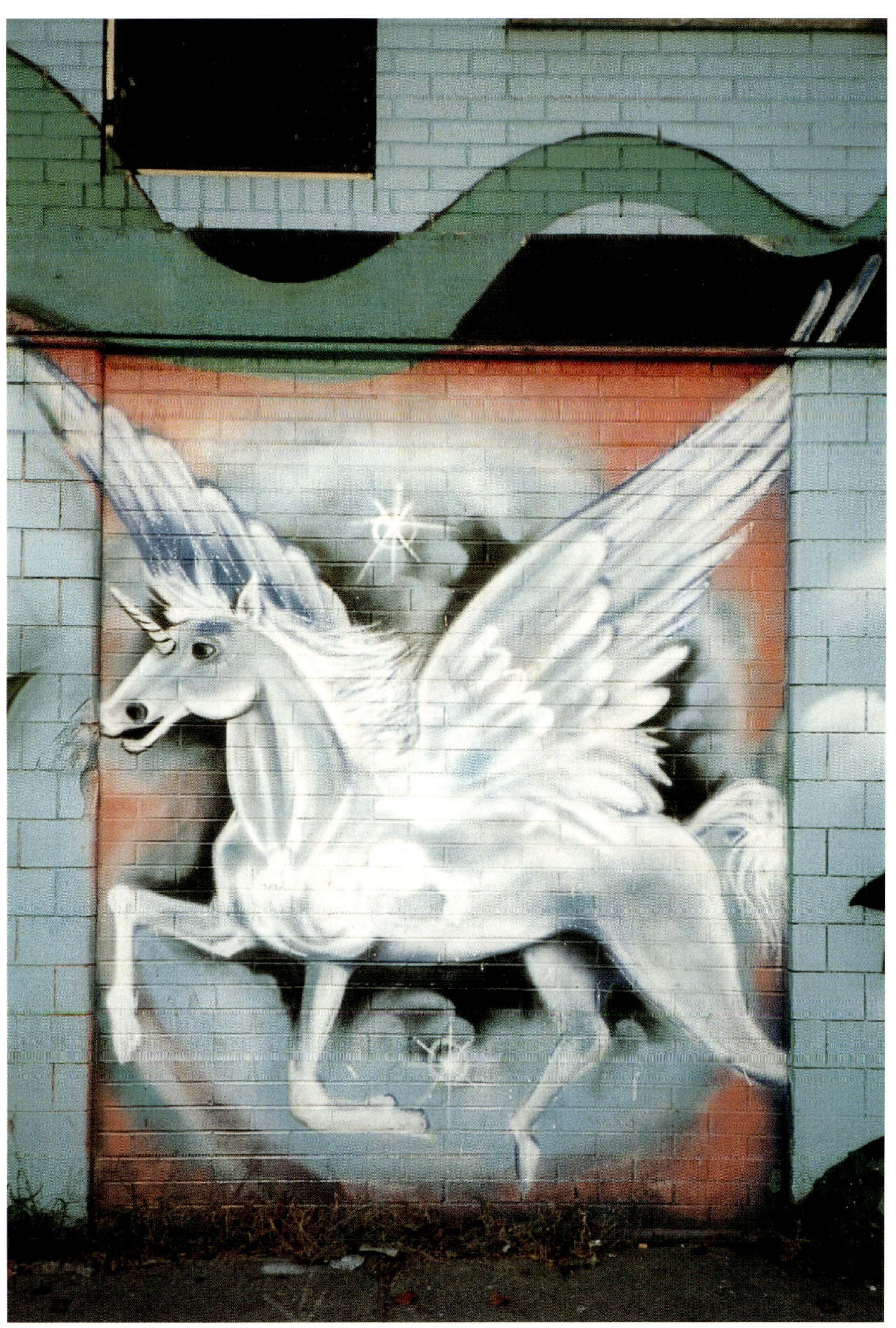

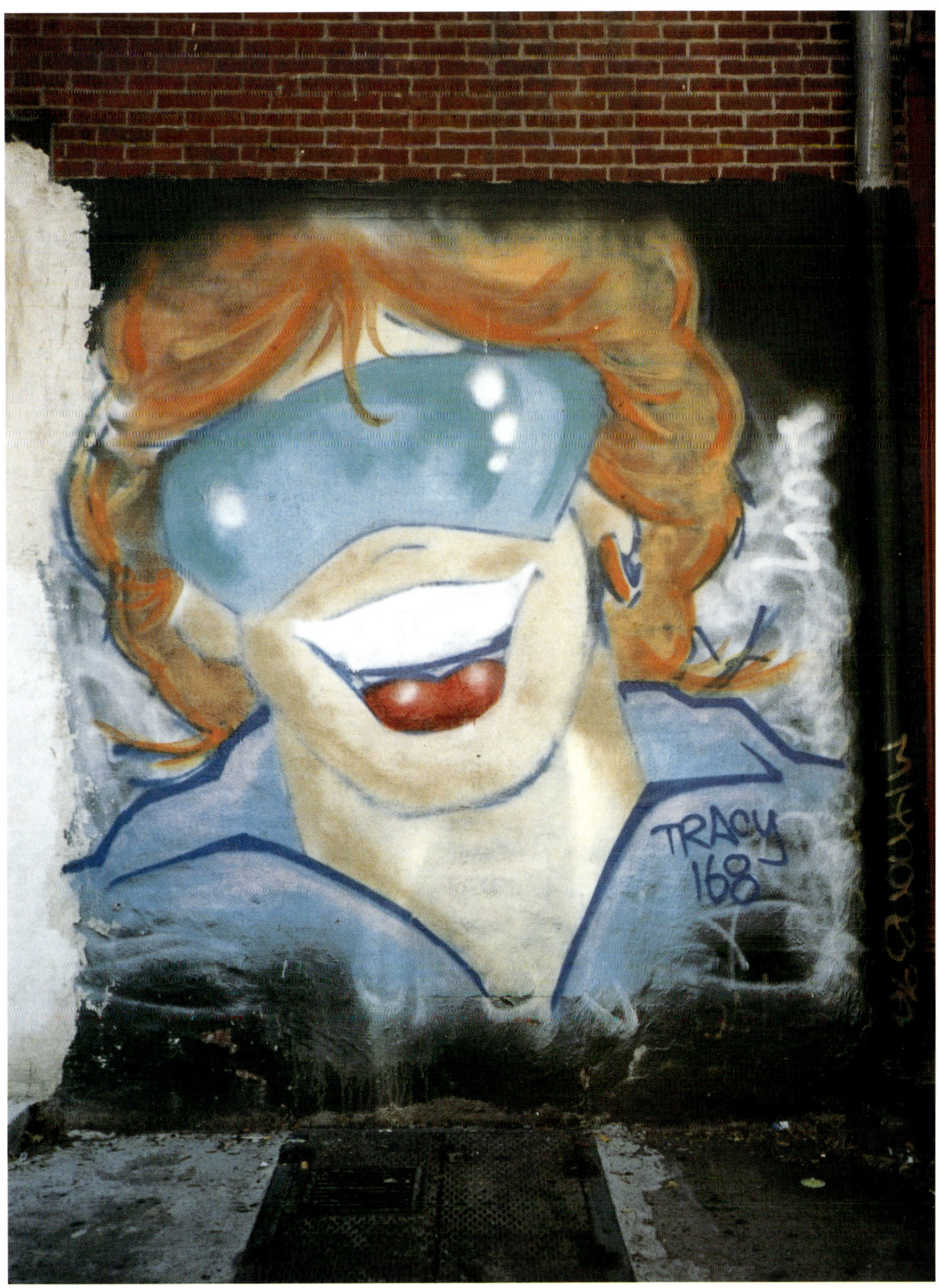

TRACY
168

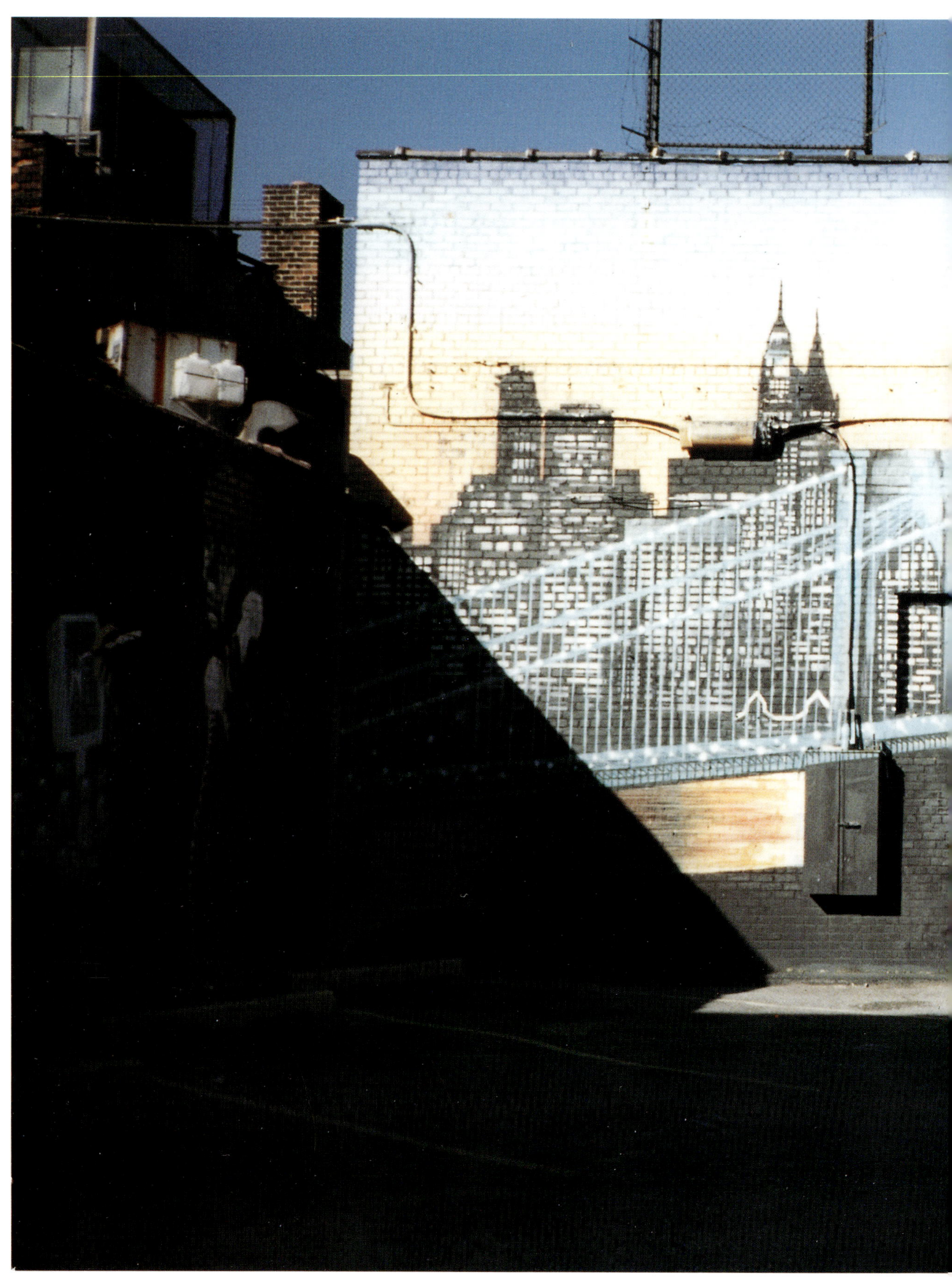

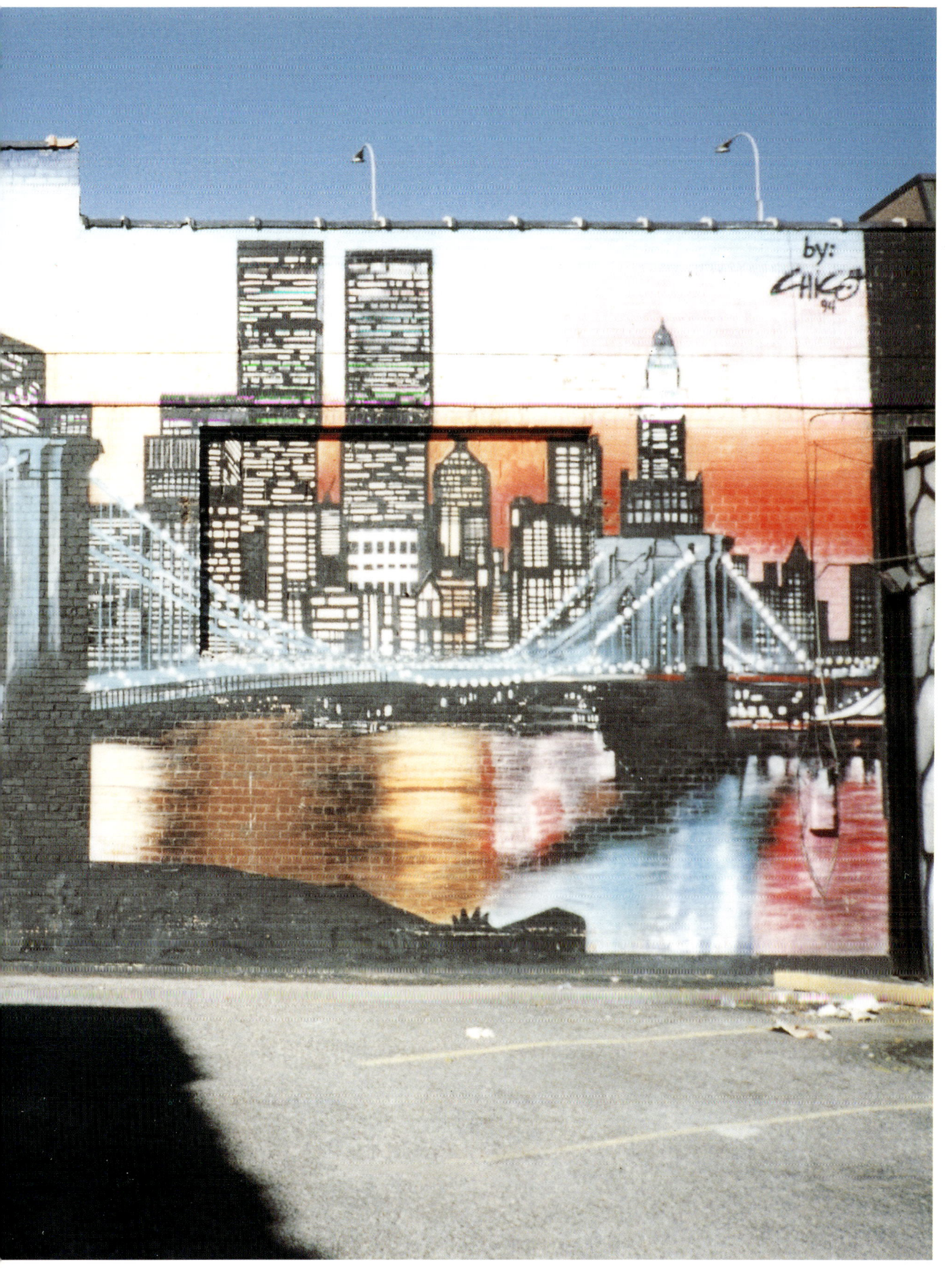
by:
CHICO
94

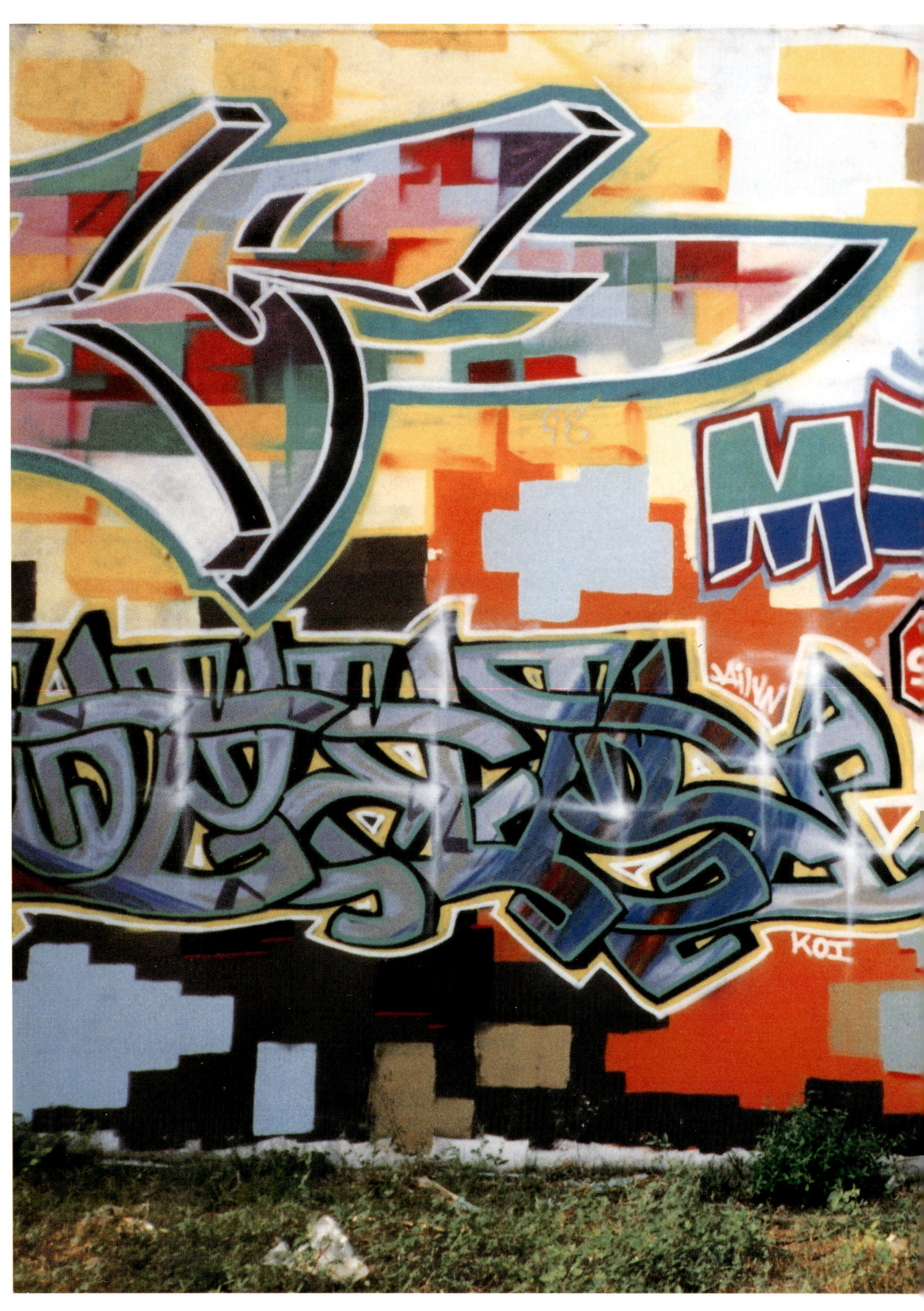

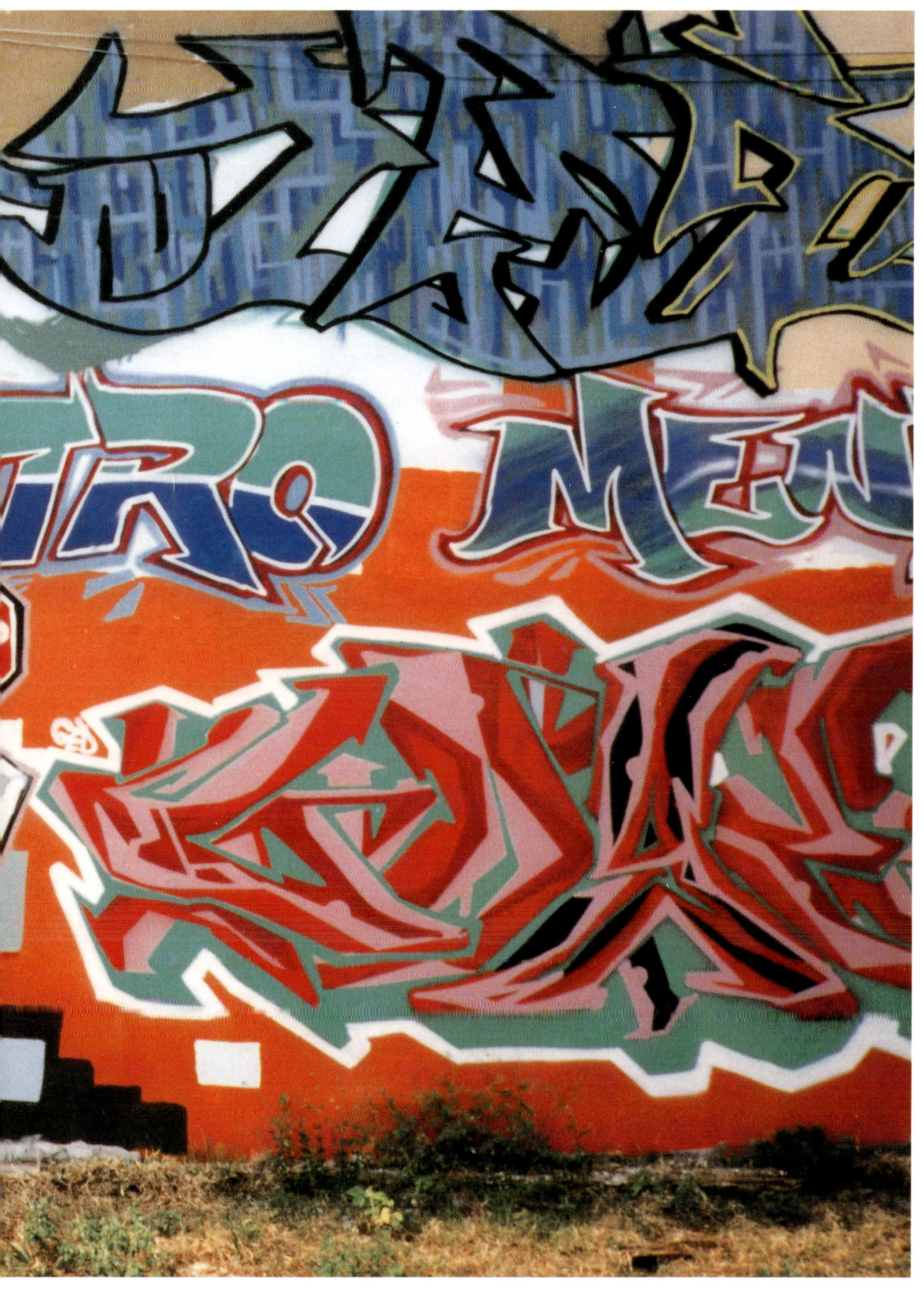

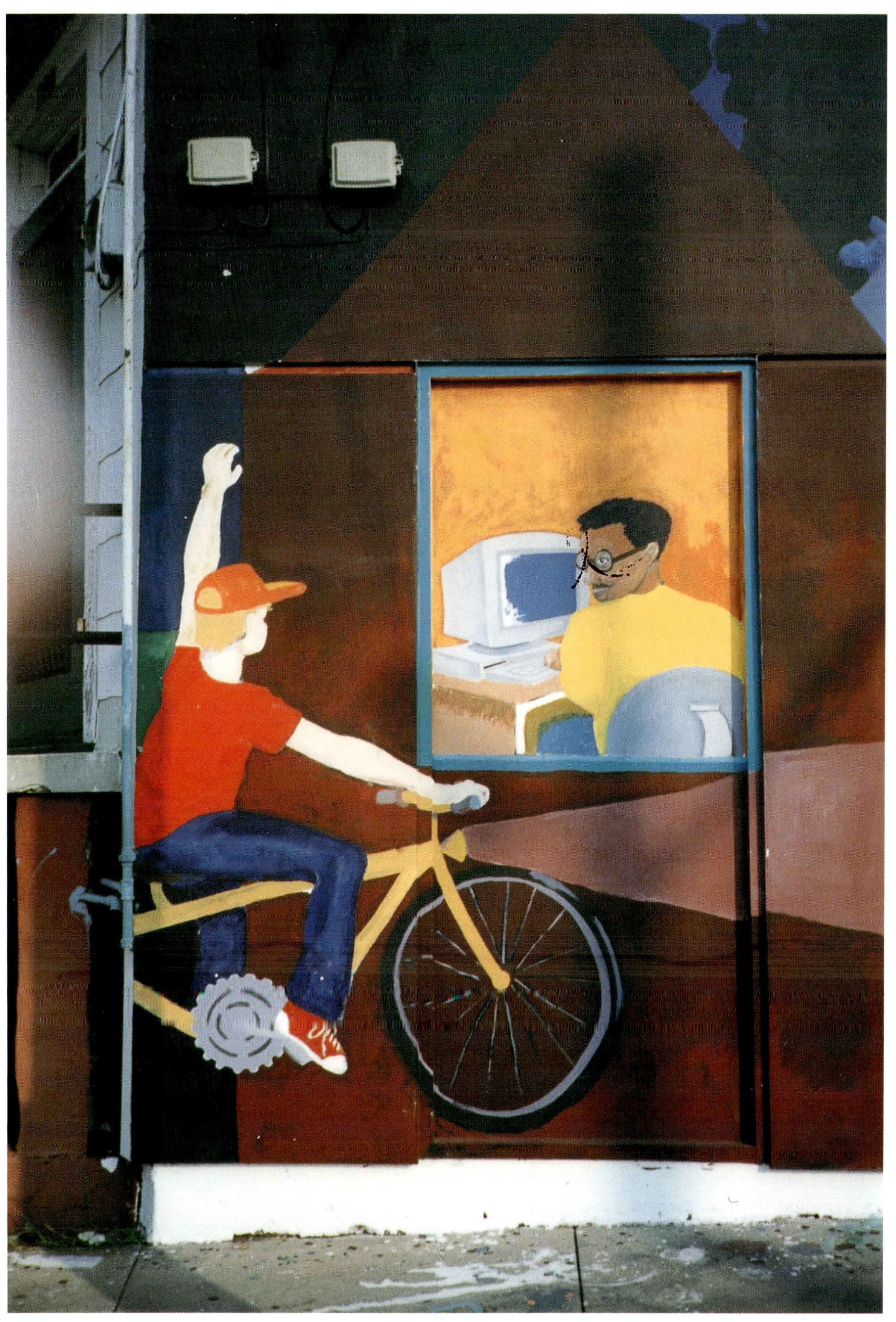

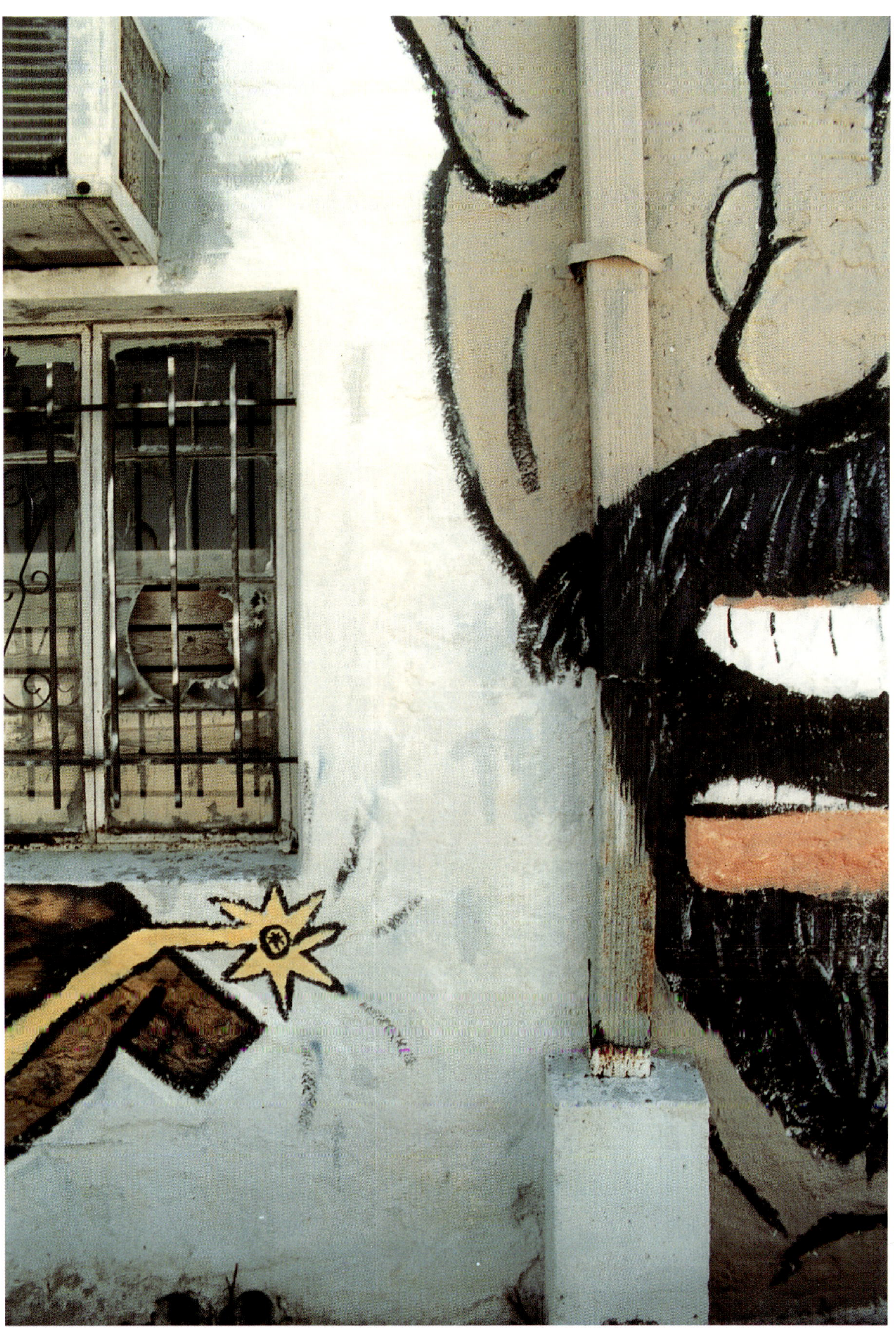

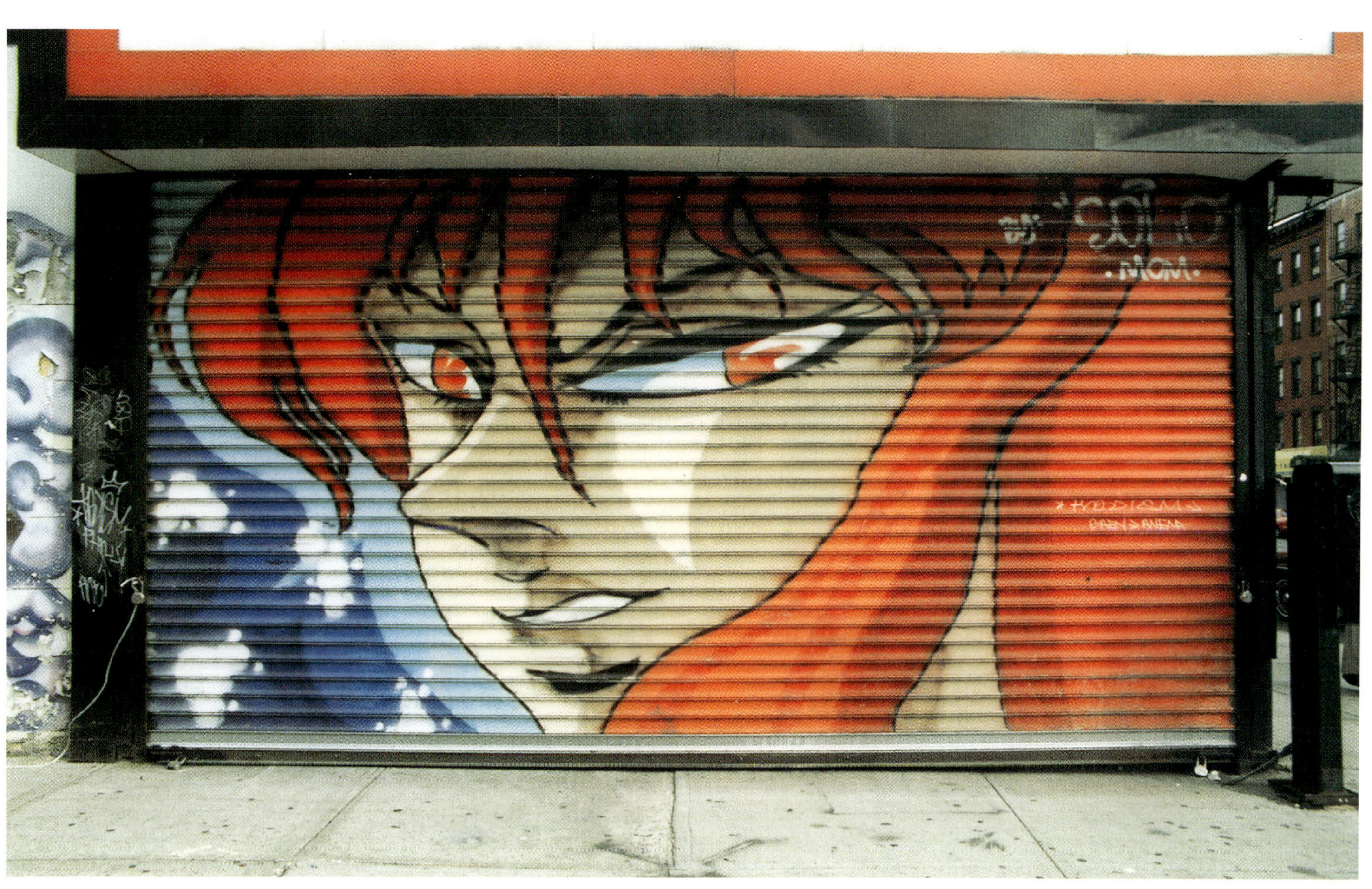

.MOM.

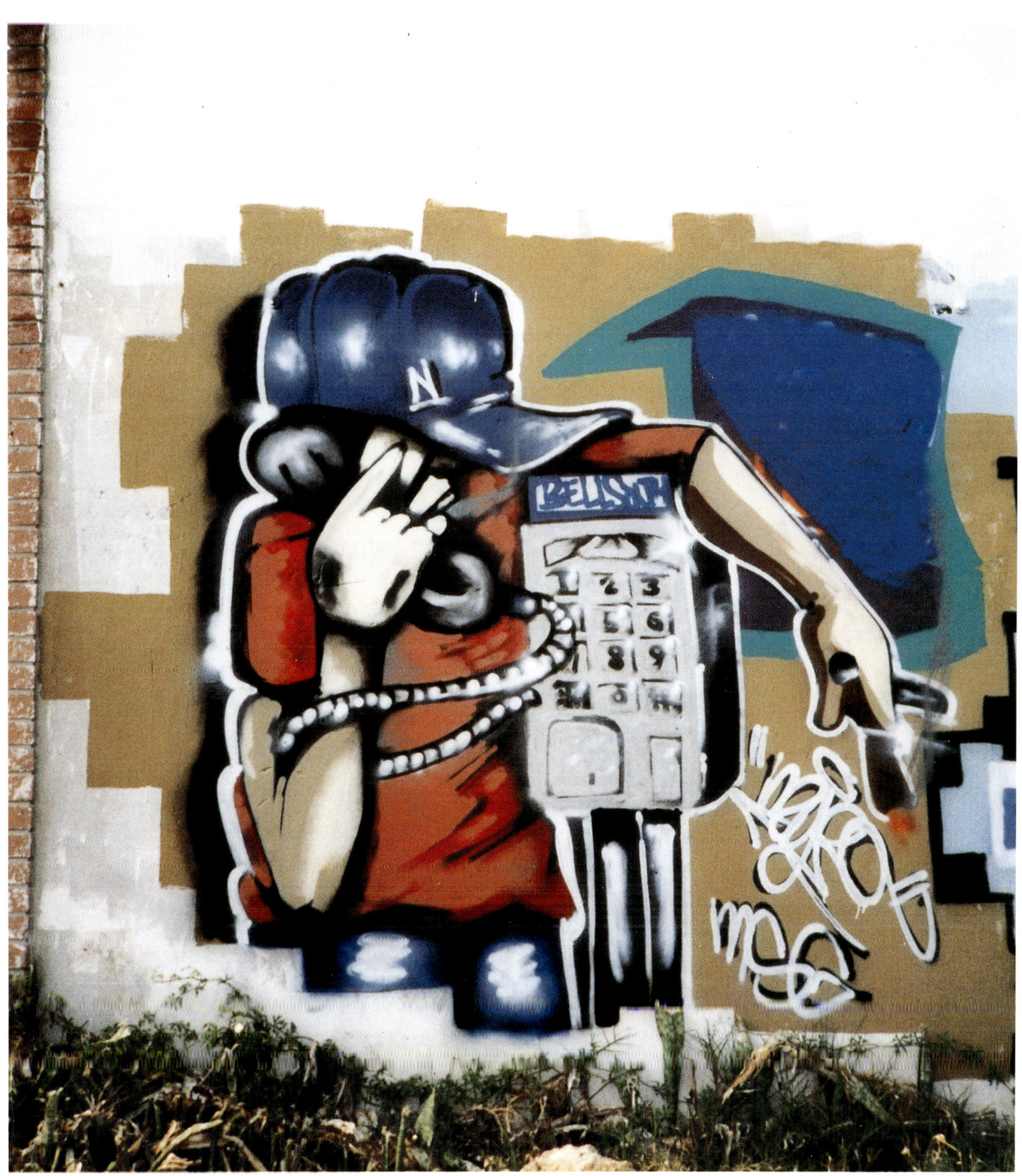

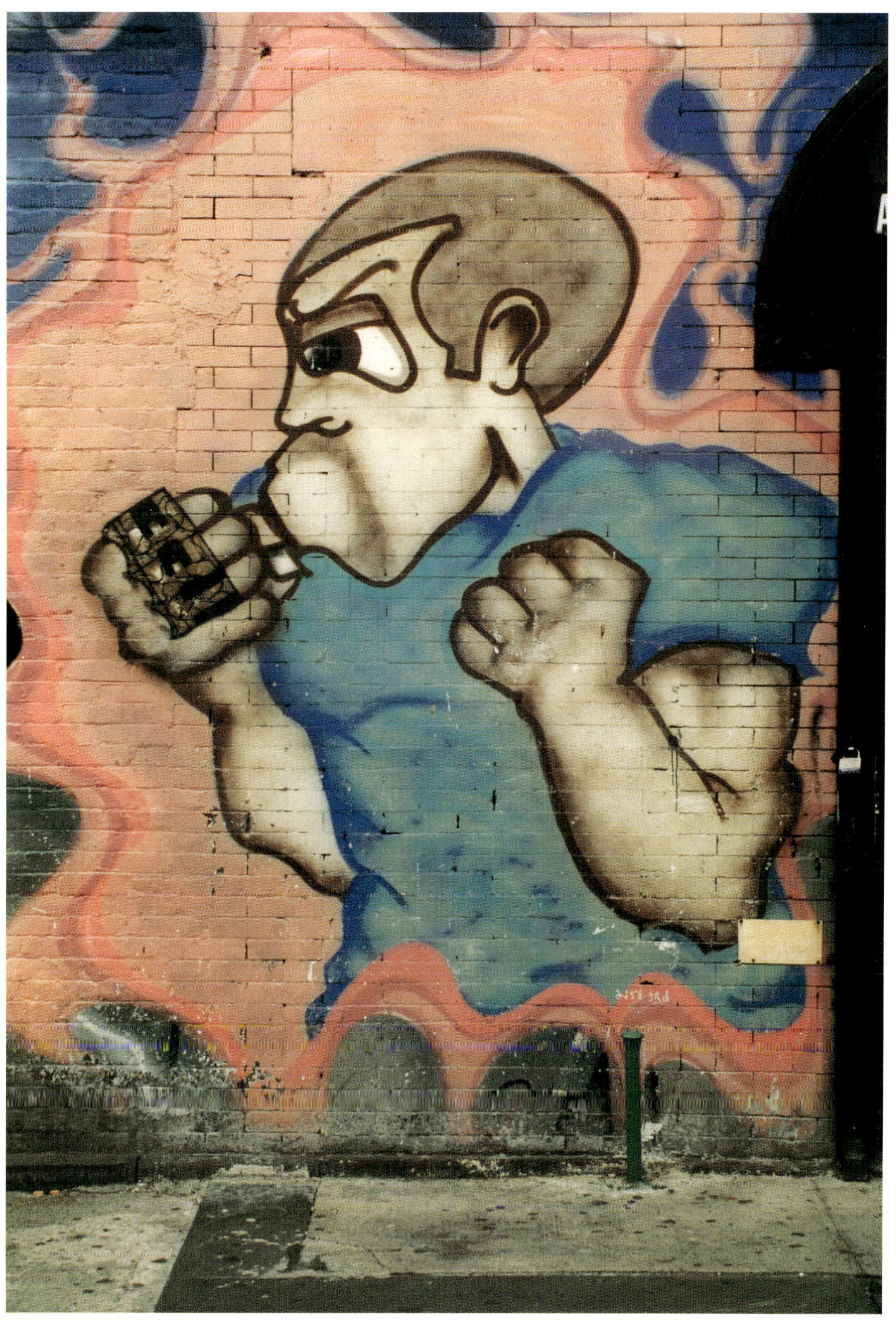

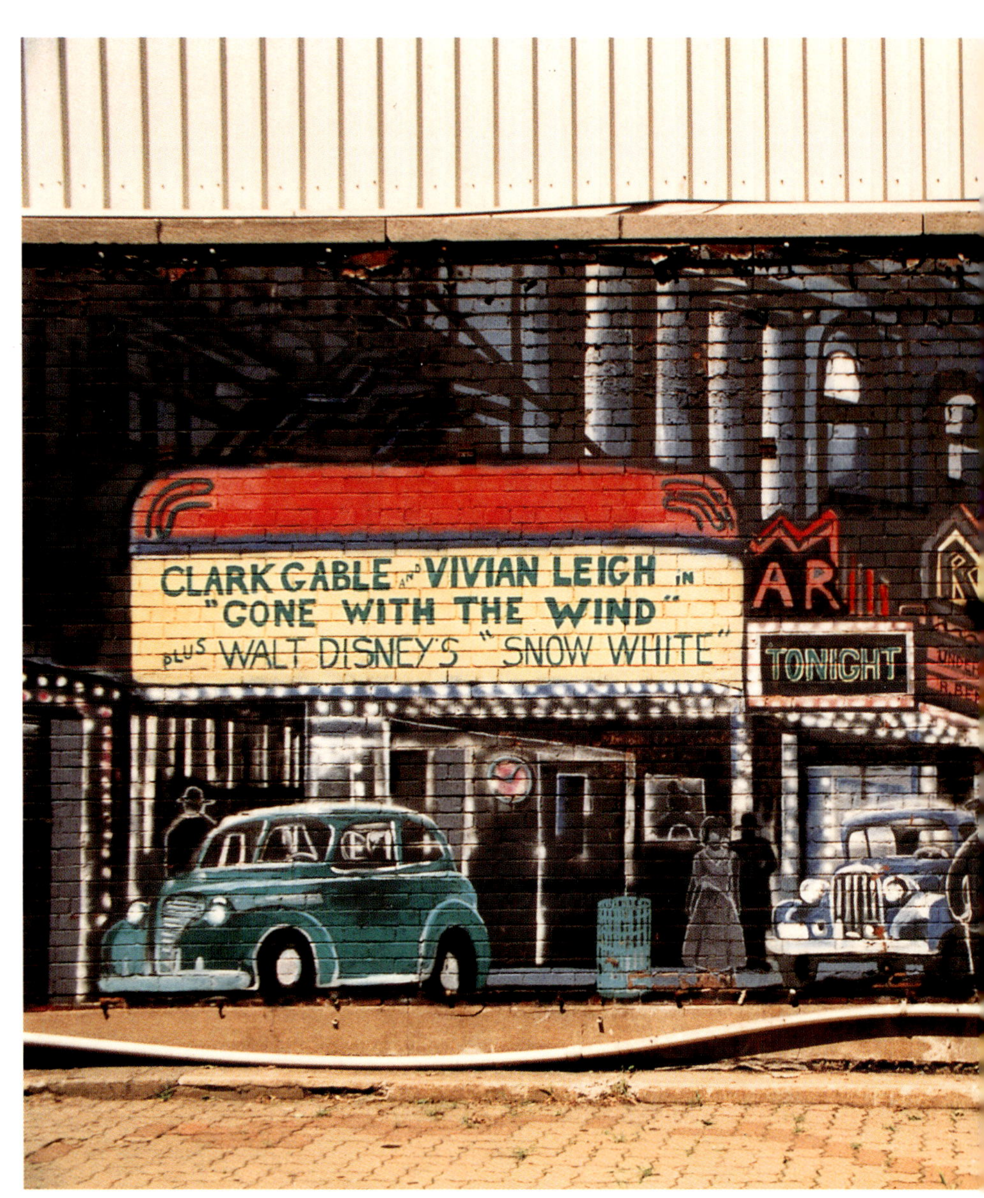

CLARK GABLE AND VIVIAN LEIGH IN
"GONE WITH THE WIND"
PLUS WALT DISNEY'S "SNOW WHITE"
TONIGHT

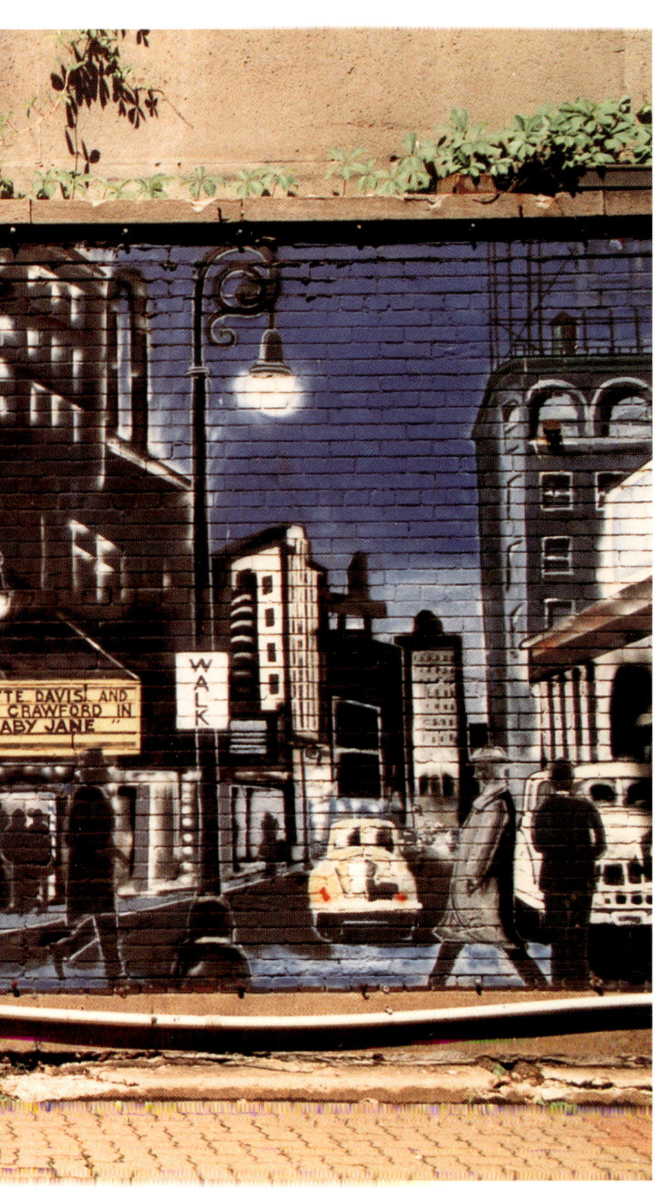
TTE DAVIS! AND
CRAWFORD IN
ABY JANE"
WALK

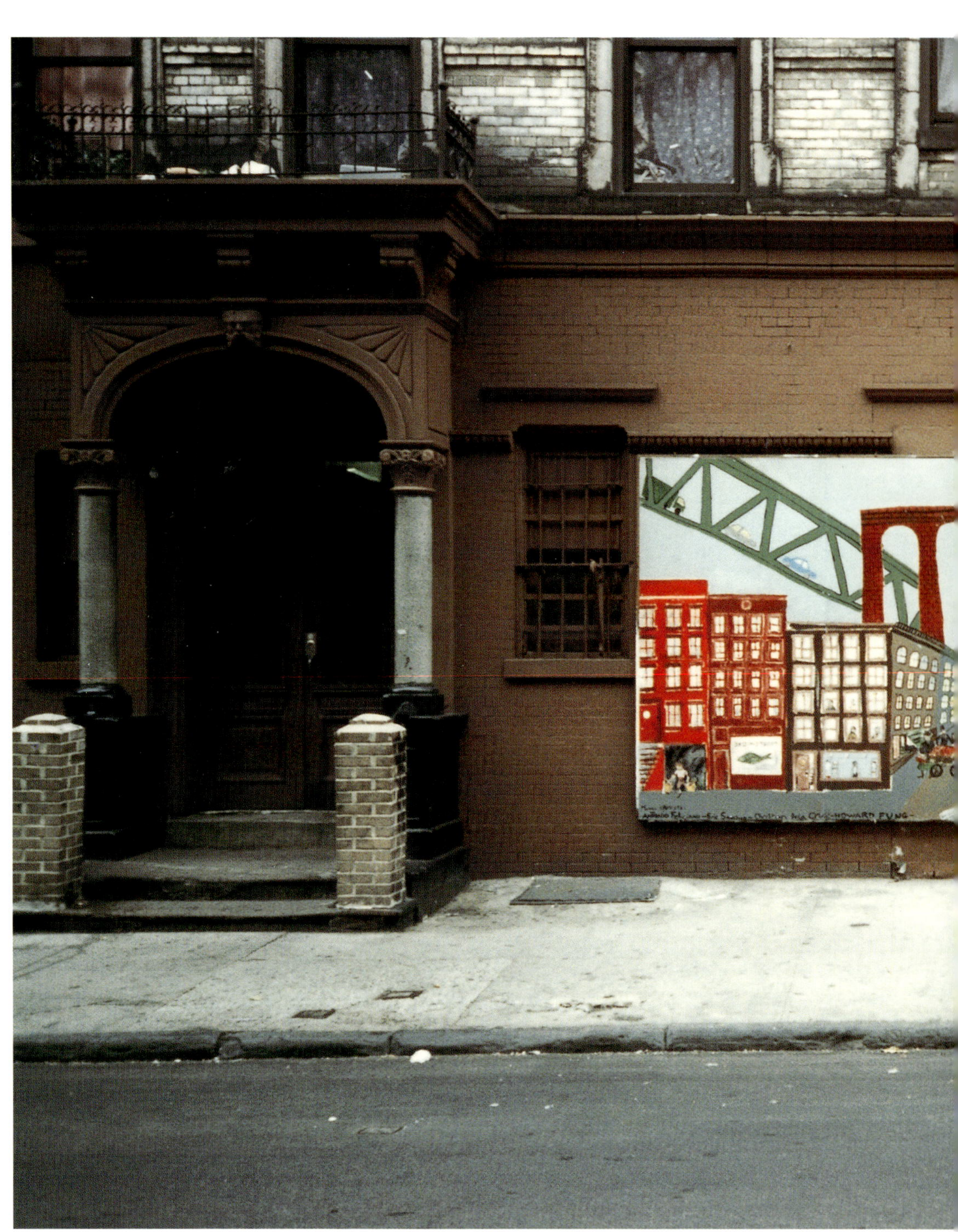

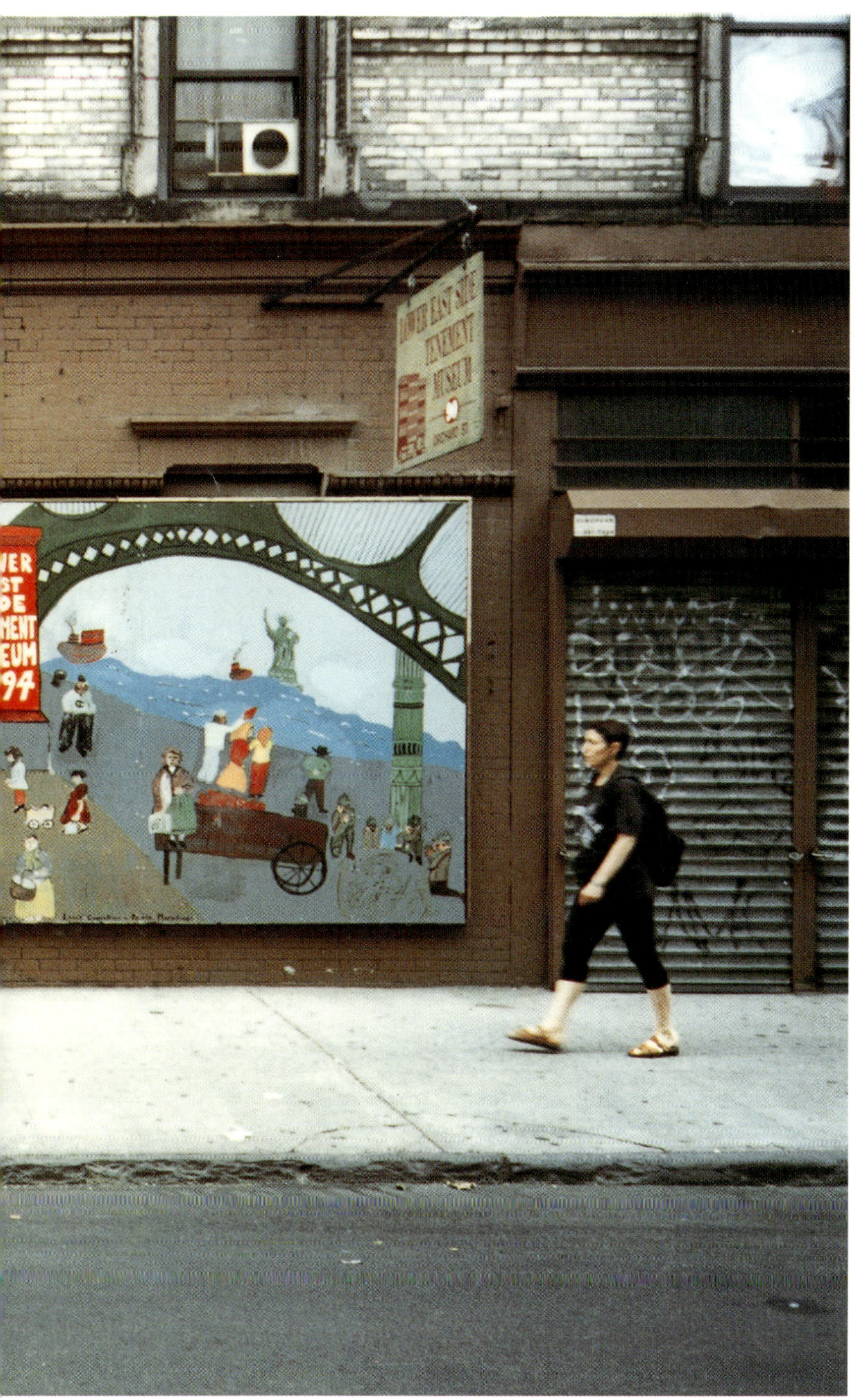

LOWER EAST SIDE
TENEMENT
MUSEUM
ORCHARD ST

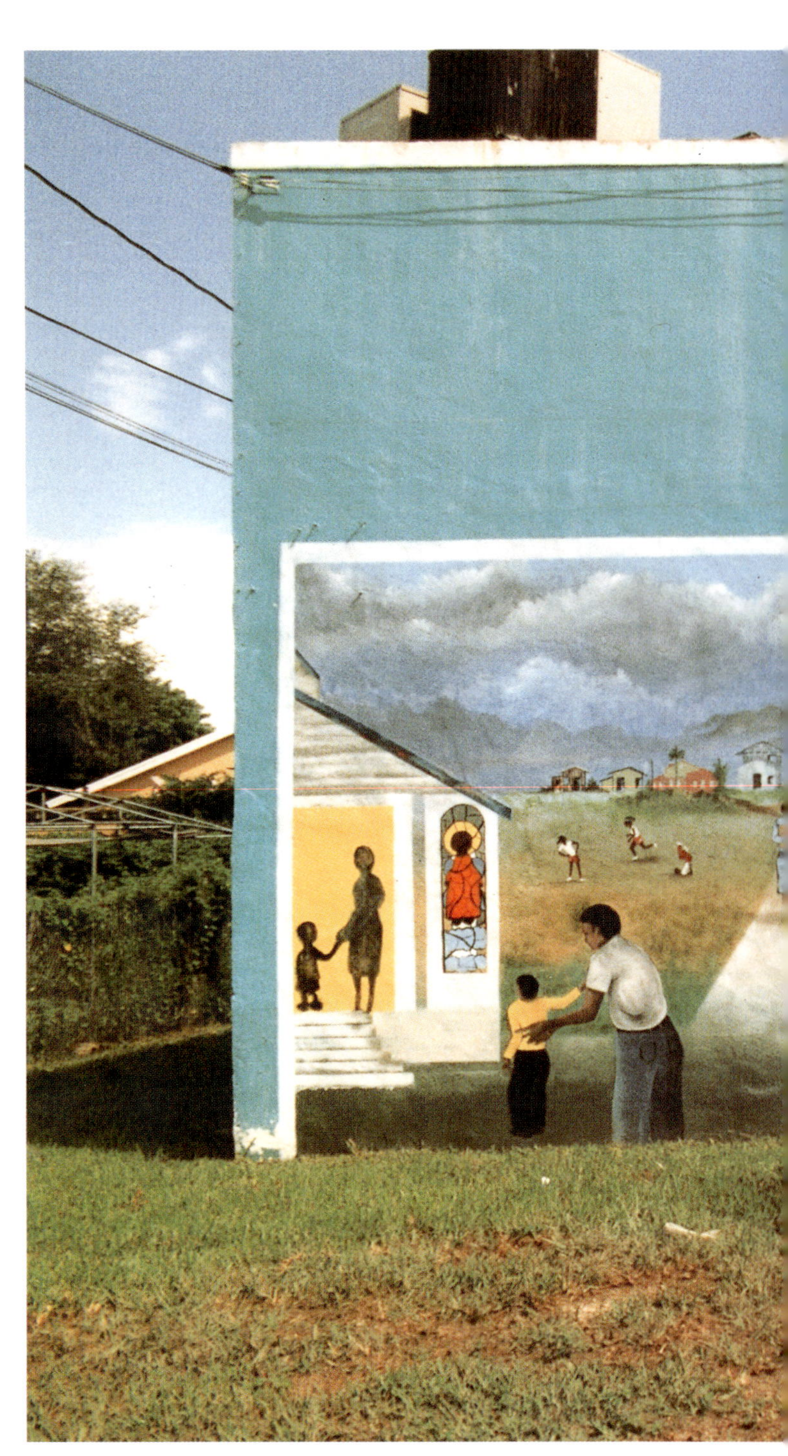

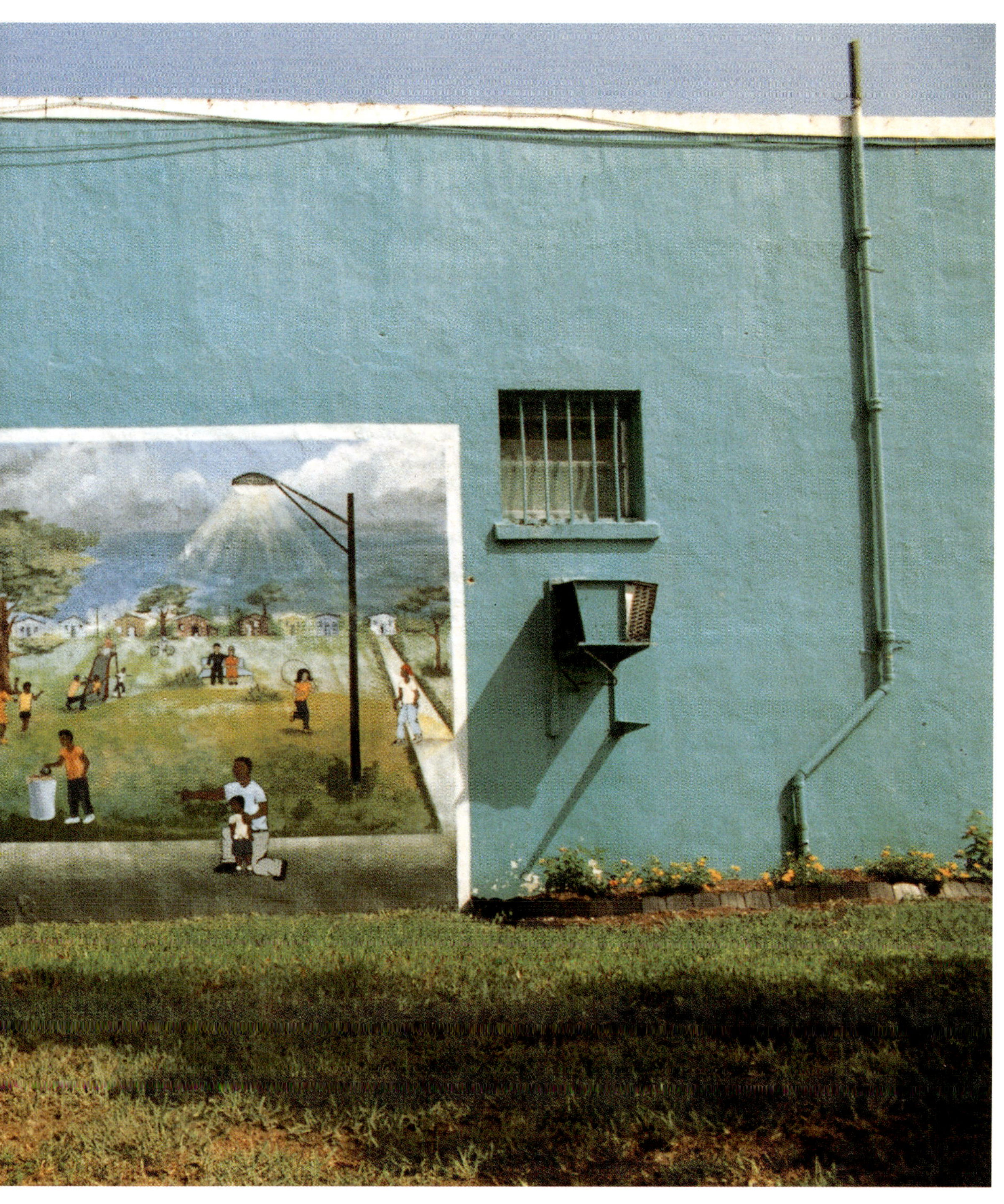

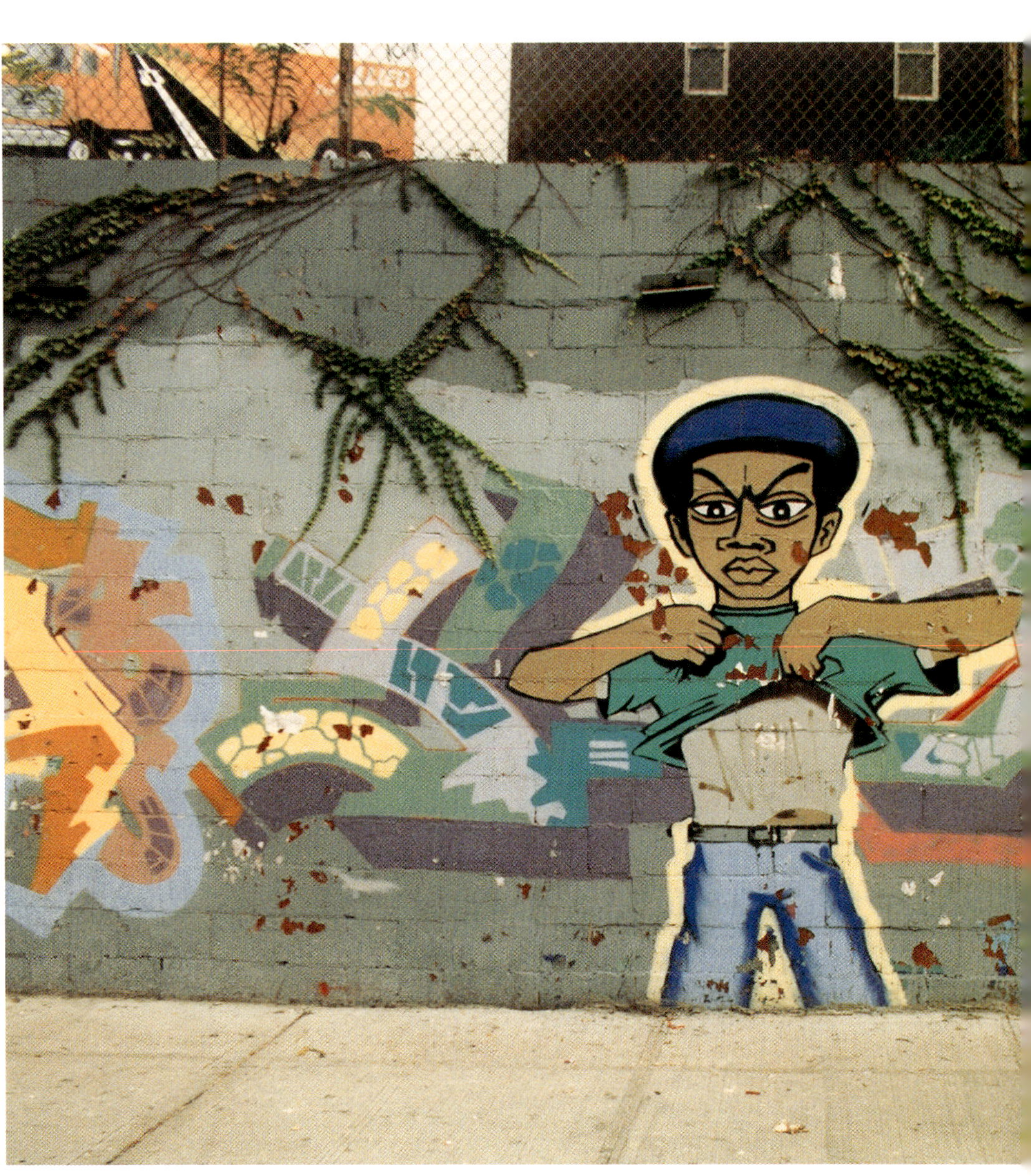

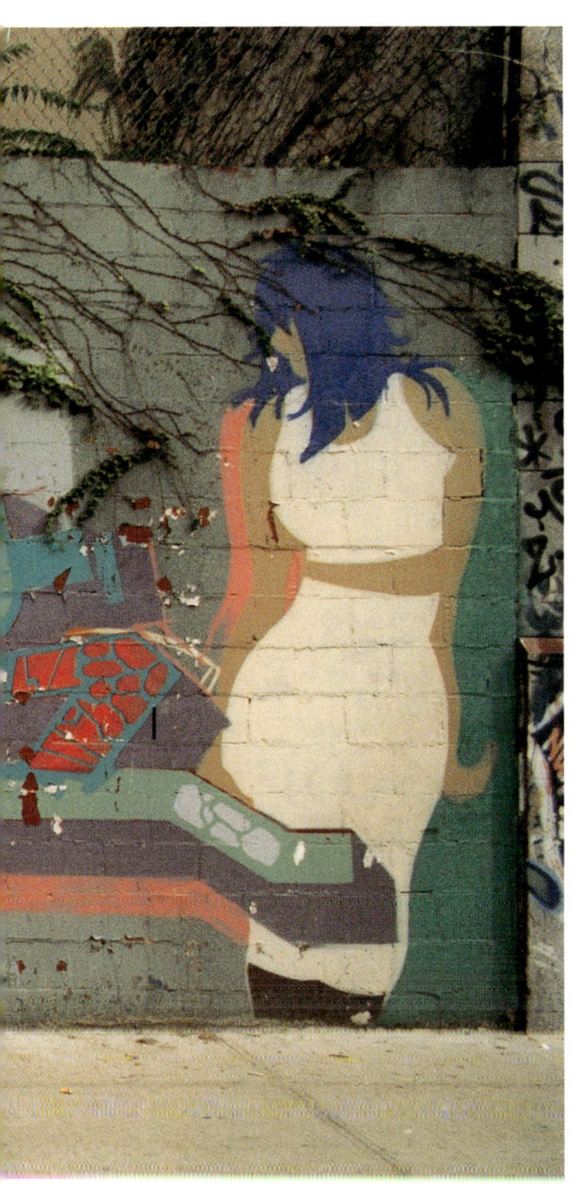

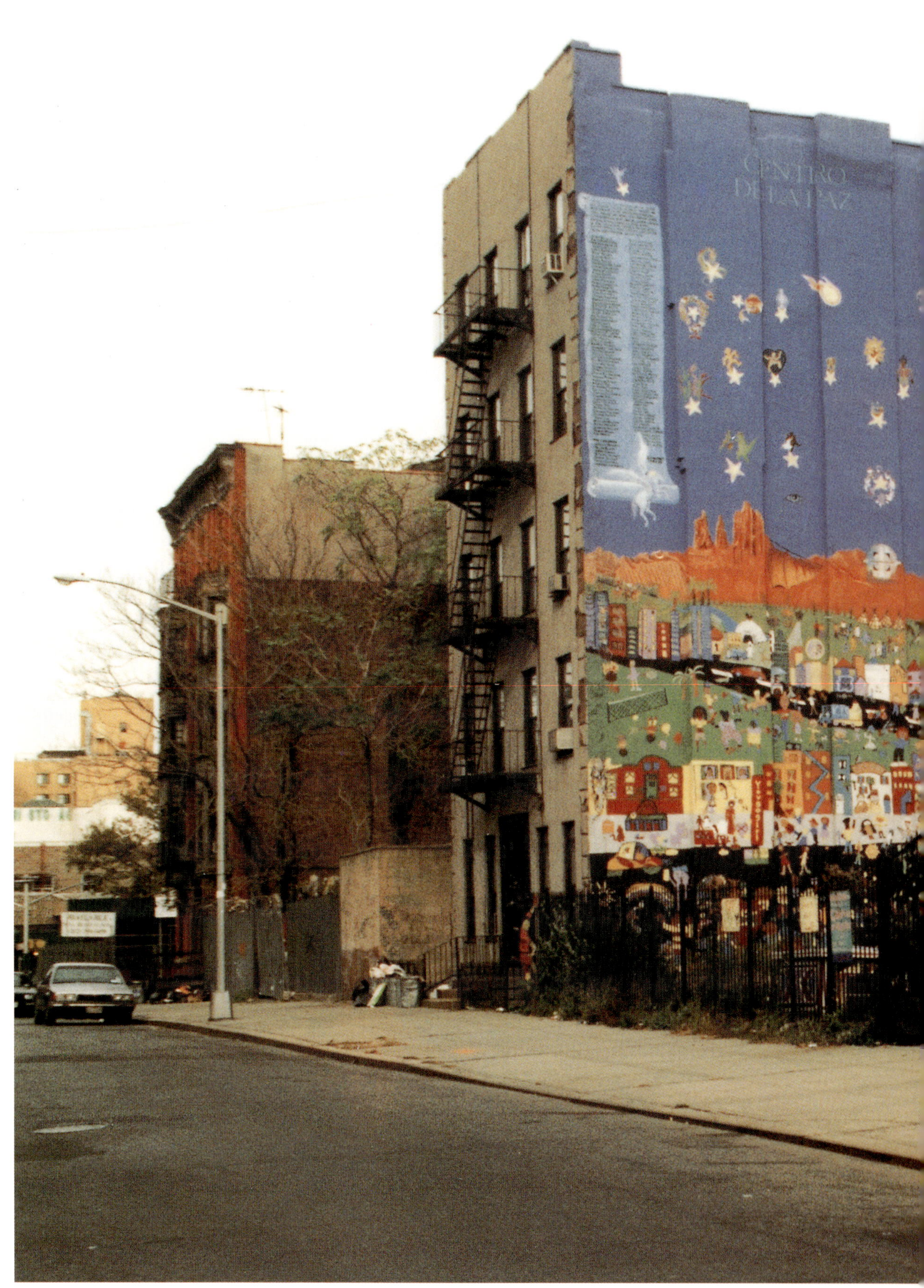

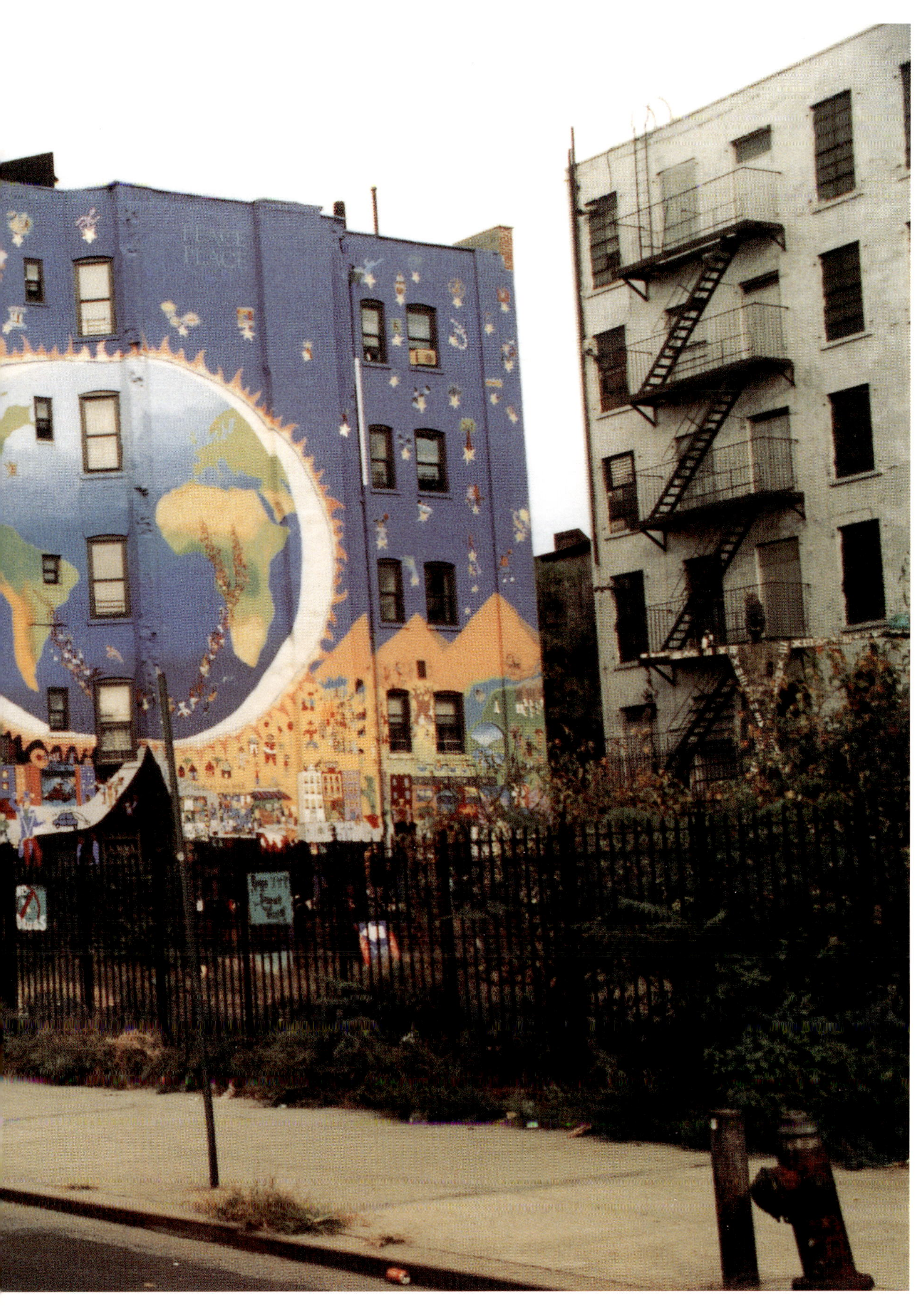

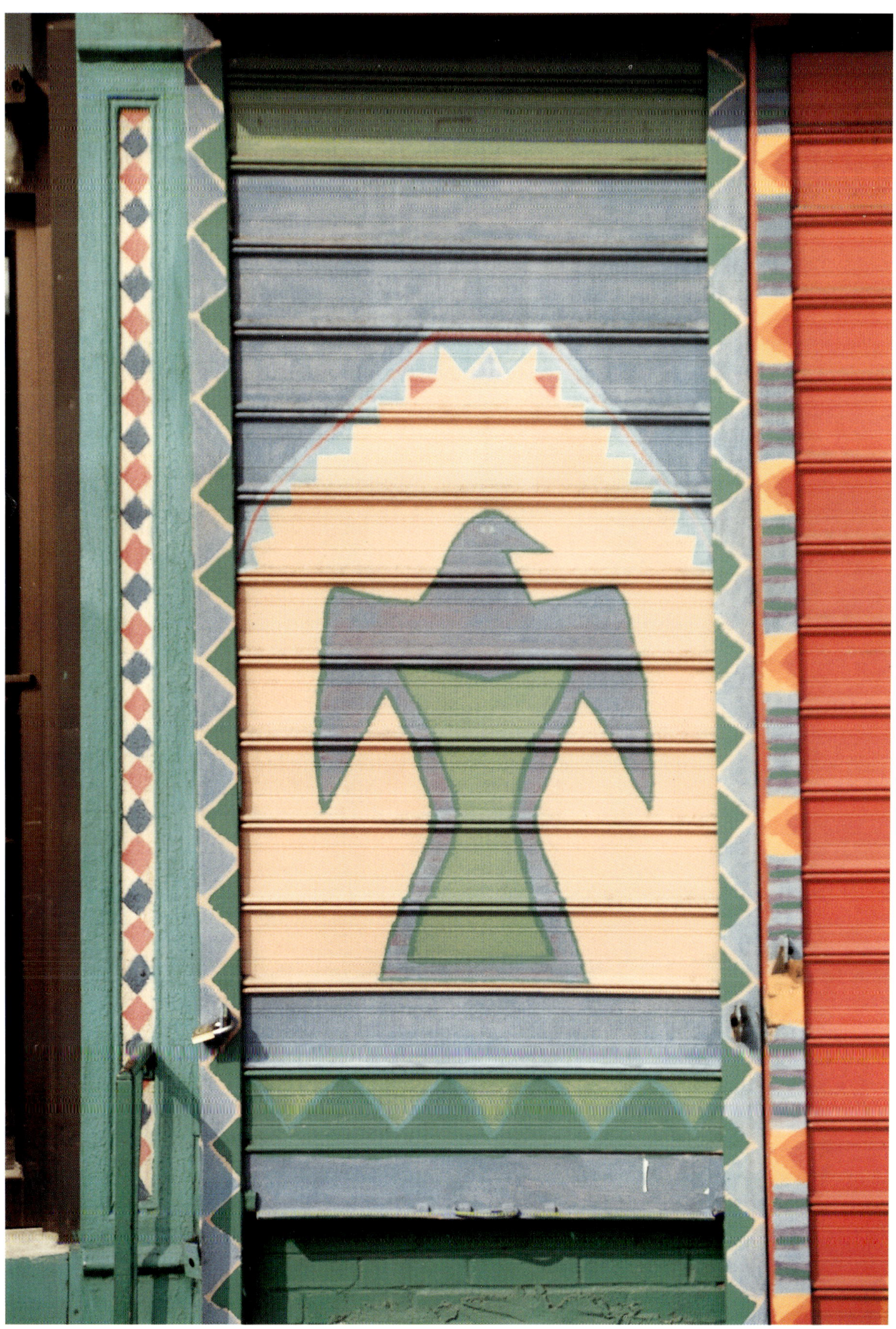

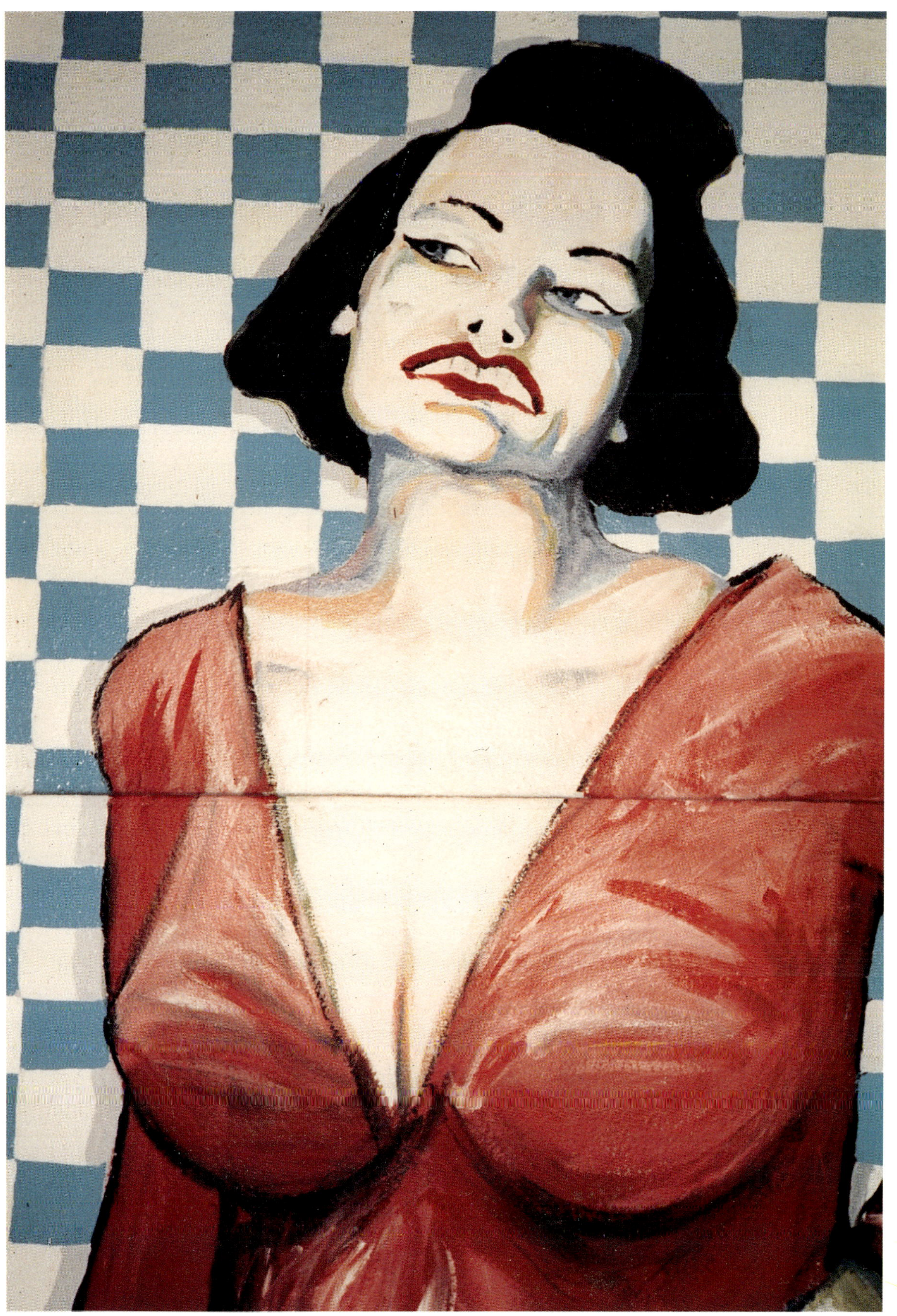

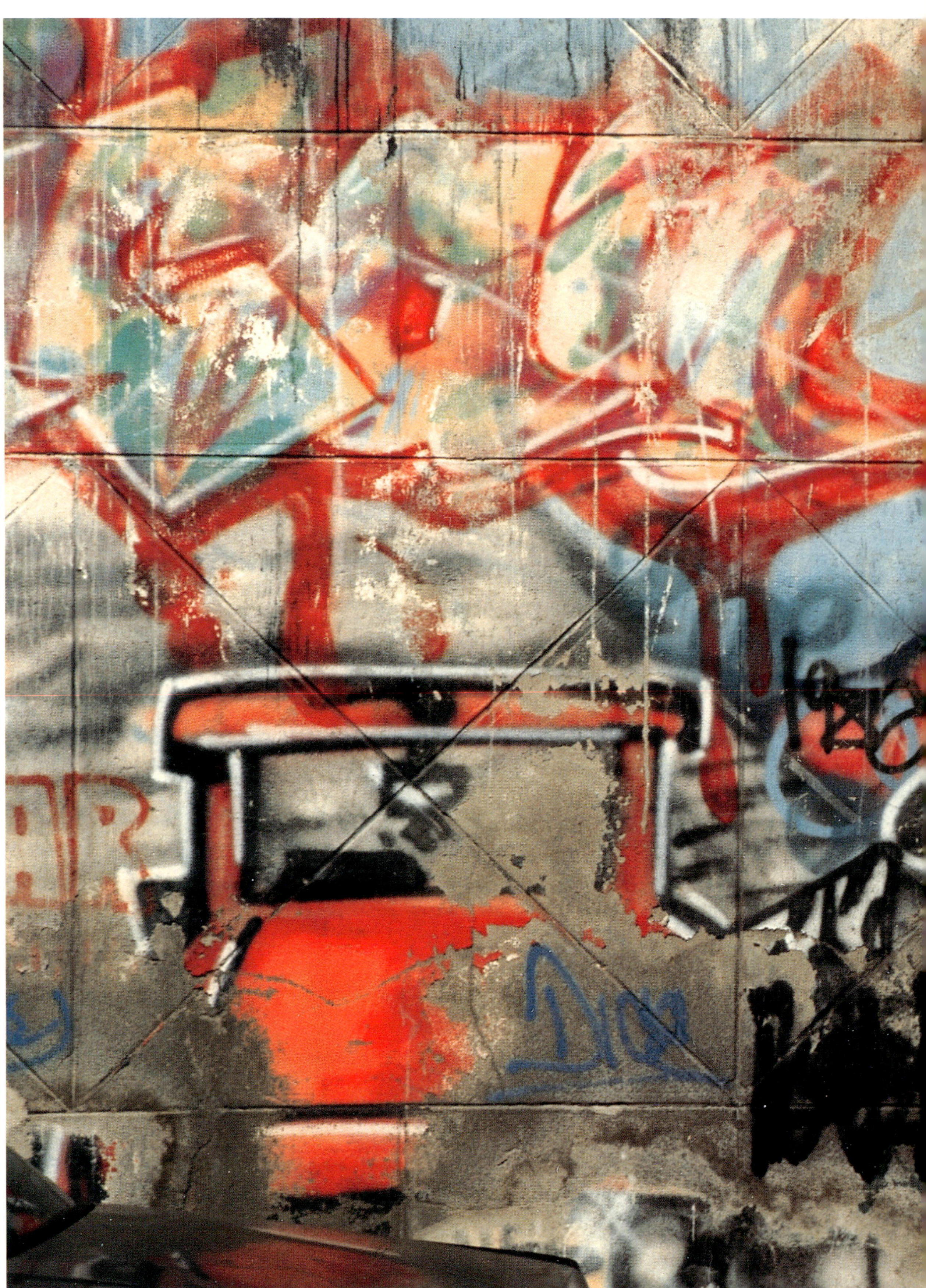

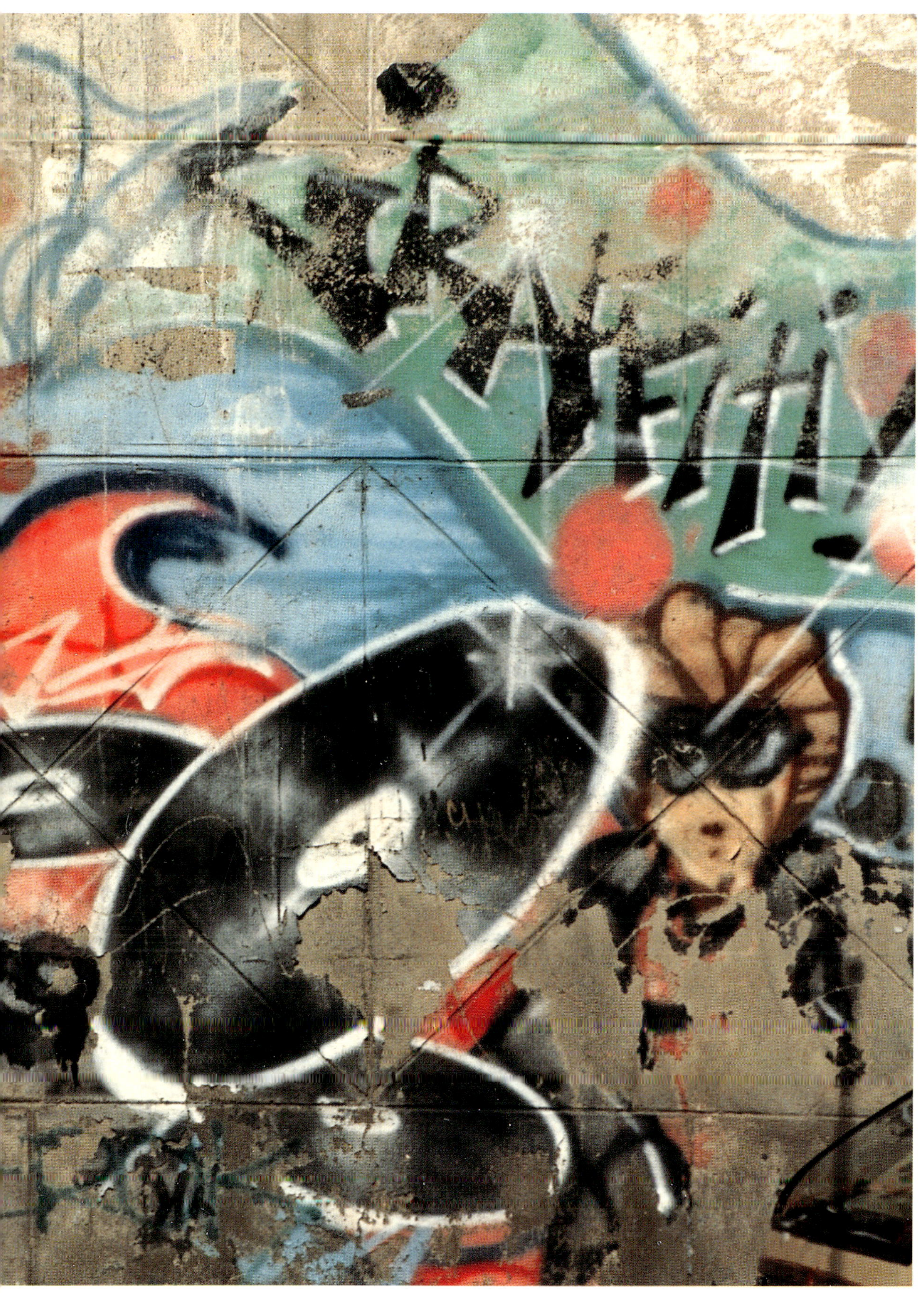

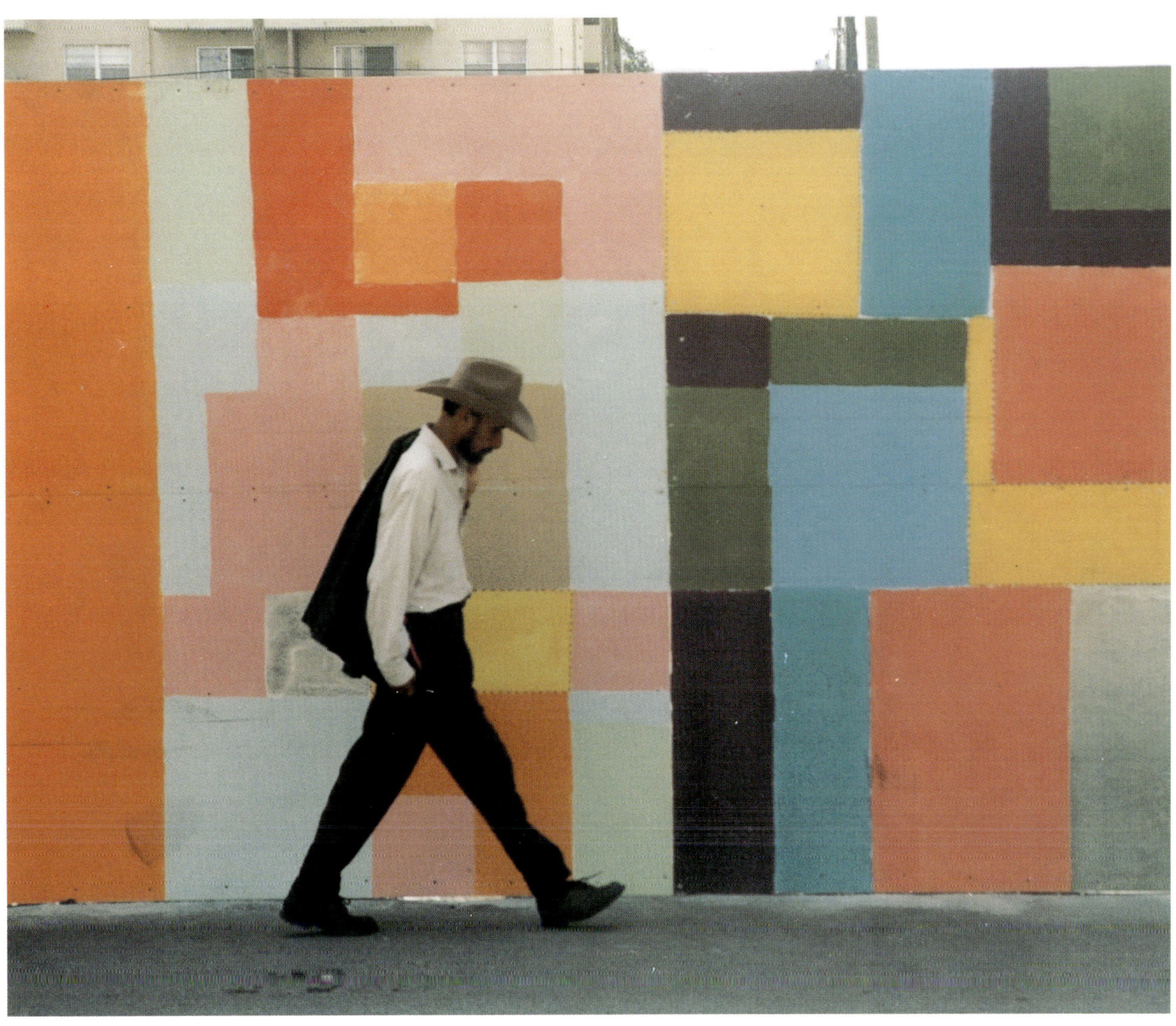

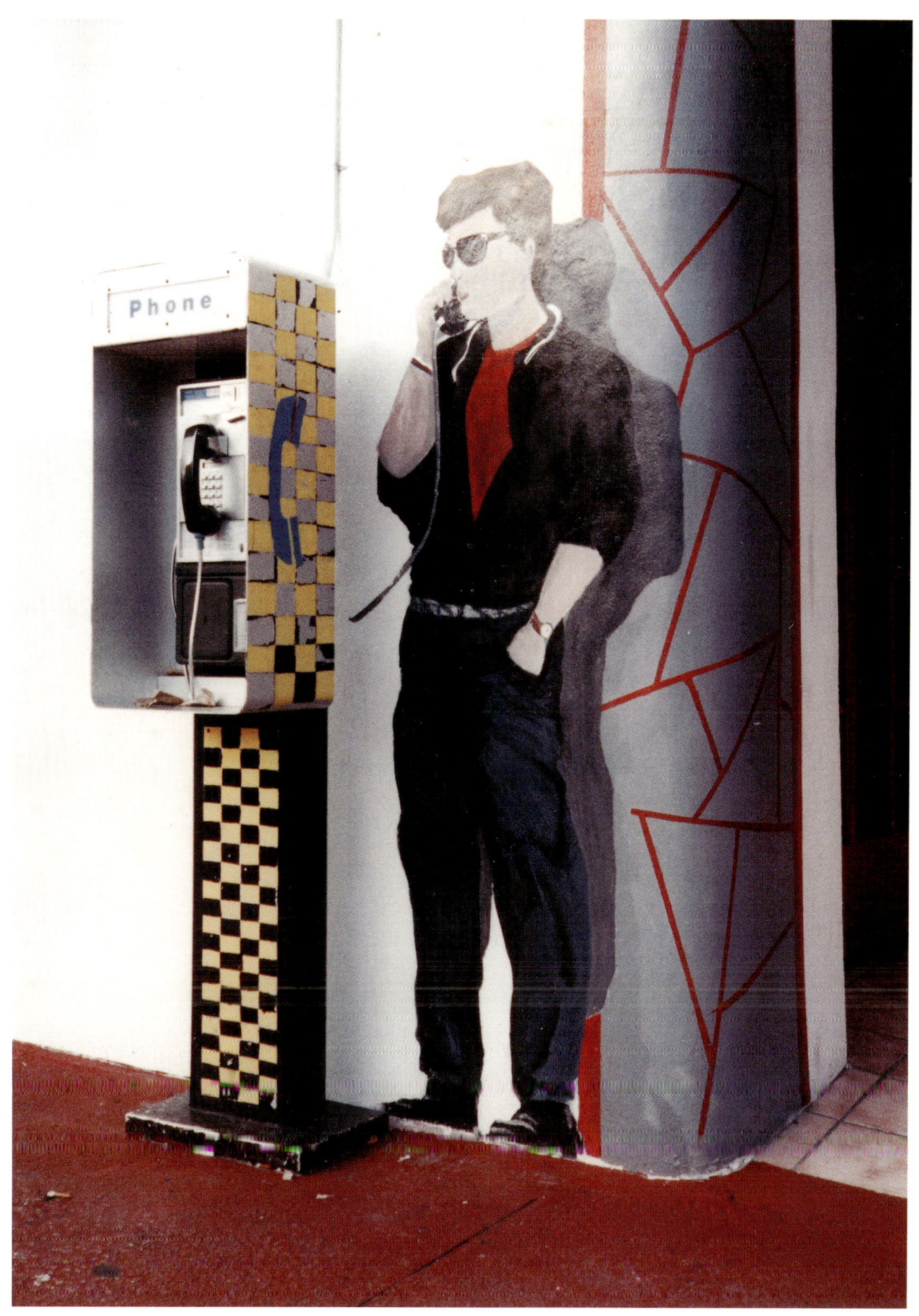

Phone

ACKNOWLEDGEMENTS

I wish I could acknowledge, individually, the many street artists who created the works that made this book possible, but I cannot, the reason being, except for a few, I have no idea who they are. A nice senario would be, the various artists see this book, get in touch with me to identify themselves, and we arrange to have them all present themselves on a major live television show, so the world would know who they are. For now, I can only express my gratitude to <u>all</u> street artists via this book and what I wrote in the introduction, expressions truly from my heart.

Following are people I do know and can acknowledge for their very significant contributions to making this book a reality: Leonard Schulman, Maureen Langer, Jim Clearwater, Steve Bornstein, and Chad Elliot. Special thanks also to brothers Art and Barry Edelson for their generous support and encouragement.

Color separations, printing and binding: C&C Offset Printing Co., Ltd., Hong Kong

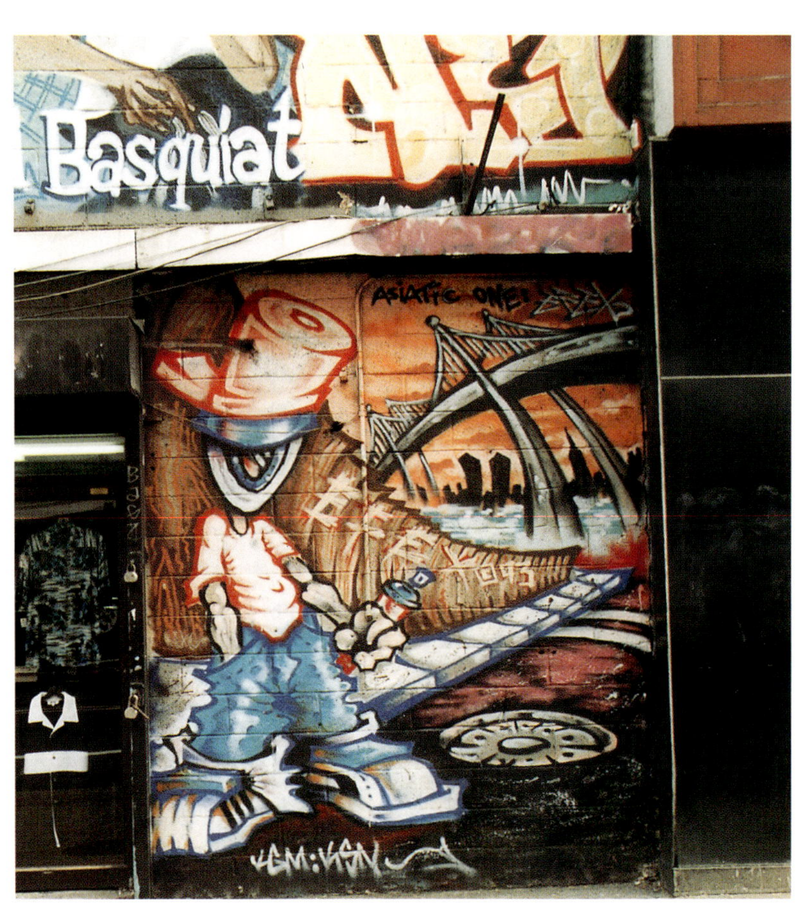
Basquiat
ASIATIC ONE